DISCOVER CANADA

Alberta

By Edna Bakken

Consultants

Desmond Morton, FRSC, Professor of History, University of Toronto

Roberta McKay, Ph.D., Faculty of Education, University of Alberta
Cheryl Craig, University of Alberta; Calgary Board of Education

 Grolier Limited
TORONTO

View of Fort Chipewyan, Alberta's oldest settlement, on the banks of Lake Athabasca
Overleaf: Mt. Temple, Banff National Park

Canadian Cataloguing in Publication Data

Bakken, Edna
  Alberta

(Discover Canada)
Rev. ed.
Includes index.
ISBN 0-7172-3047-3

1. Alberta — Juvenile literature. I. Title.
II. Series: Discover Canada (Toronto, Ont.).

FC3661.2.B35 1993   971.23   C94-930097-7
F1076.4.B35 1993

Front cover: Indian paintbrush and other wild-flowers carpet the floor of a mountain canyon.
Back cover: ''Nodding donkey'' oil pump near Longview, south of Calgary

Printed and bound in Canada.
Published simultaneously in the United States.
1 2 3 4 5 6 7 8 9 10   DWF   99 98 97 96 95 94 93 92 91

The Bow River as it winds its way through Banff National Park

Table of Contents

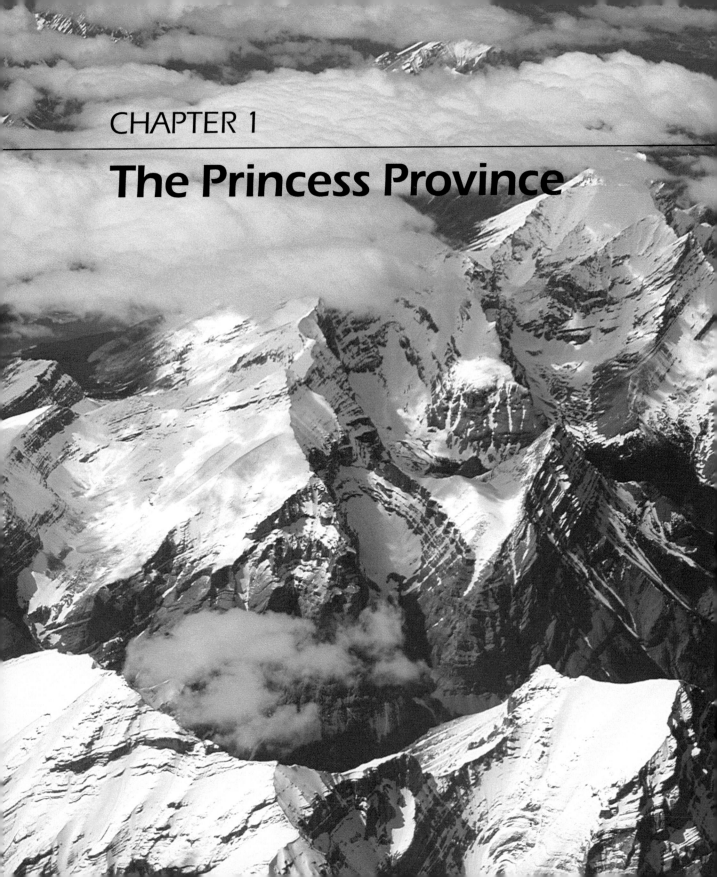

CHAPTER 1
The Princess Province

Alberta is sometimes called the Princess Province. This seems an appropriate name for a province that has an abundance of natural beauty, wealth and cultures, and was named for Princess Louise Caroline Alberta, daughter of Queen Victoria.

The landscape is Alberta's greatest source of beauty. Along the southwestern border, like a crown, stretch the magnificent snow-capped Rocky Mountains. At the base of the Rockies, the forested foothills ripple out toward the prairie. Melting glaciers drain away through three major river systems and hundreds of lakes fill the landscape's dimples. Alpine meadows, forests and grasslands support many species of birds and animals.

Alberta's wealth has come from the development of its natural resources. The Native peoples lived on the abundant plants and animals in the area. European fur traders gathered a wealth of animal pelts. Ranchers added riches when they moved cattle into the foothills in the 1880s. Homesteaders cleared trees and dug into the prairie to produce grain. The forest industry was born when timber was needed to build homes and towns. Discoveries of coal, oil and natural gas heaped more treasure on the province.

The province's strength lies in its people, who weave the vitality of several cultures into the fabric of the province. Many people who call Alberta home keep their original traditions and customs alive even as they create new ones to fit life in the Princess Province.

Aerial view of the Canadian Rocky Mountains

CHAPTER 2

The Land

Located between the 110th and 120th meridians of west longitude, Alberta is the most western of the three Prairie Provinces: Manitoba, Saskatchewan and Alberta. With an area of 661 185 square kilometres (255 285 square miles), Alberta covers one-fifteenth of Canada's land area. It is the fourth largest province. Except for the southwest corner, Alberta is roughly rectangular in shape. Provincial boundaries measure 3926 kilometres (2440 miles). Alberta's location as an inland province, situated great distances from any coastline, provides government, agriculture and industry with transportation and economic challenges.

Topography

Alberta has four natural features: mountains, foothills, plains and the Canadian Shield. Except for the highest mountain peaks, the Cypress Hills and parts of the Porcupine Hills, these natural features were shaped by the last ice age. As the ice sheet receded, it dumped deposits of clay, sand and boulders, which were left in long piles, or moraines. Lakes, sloughs and potholes formed when moraines blocked the run-off from the melting ice. The Columbia Ice Fields, Athabasca, Saskatchewan and Columbia glaciers are remnants of the ice sheet.

The Rocky Mountains are one chain in the massive Cordillera (kor dill yair' uh) that extends through North and South America. The highest point in Alberta is Mount Columbia which rises to

Overleaf: **Grain fields near Longview in Alberta's renowned foothills country**

Elk Creek, a clear, gravel-bottomed stream favoured by the Dolly Varden, an imaginatively named species of trout. *Inset, left*: The Athabasca Glacier juts out from the main body of the Columbia Icefield, a remnant of the vast sheet of ice that once covered most of Canada. *Inset, right*: A pothole formed as the ice sheet receded

3747 metres (12 293 feet). Although much of the Rocky Mountain region is still wilderness, people have made an imprint. Towns, railways and highways have been carved into the Rockies. Many mountain towns developed near natural resources such as limestone, coal and timber. Jasper, Banff and Lake Louise (at 1540 metres — 5052 feet — the highest town in Canada) evolved to serve visitors to Canada's first national parks. Railways and paved highways carry traffic through the Rocky Mountains via the Crowsnest, Yellowhead and Kicking Horse passes.

Alberta's foothills, the long ridges that occur between the mountains and plains, are heavily forested. Many foothill towns produce paper and wood products. Pincher Creek, Turner Valley and Black Diamond tap into the oil and gas reserves beneath the glacial moraines.

About three-quarters of the province is flat plain broken by deep river valleys and coulees, or dry gulches. In some places, flat-topped high hills stand from 200 to 750 metres (650 to 2500 feet) above the prairie. Forest and muskeg cover much of the northern plains. Most of Alberta's cities are located on the plains, which also contain the best farmland. This means that population centres and farmers often compete for the same land.

The Canadian Shield, a vast ring of rock that covers much of North America, is located above ground in some parts of the continent and underground in others. In Alberta, the Shield appears

Top: **Gently rolling prairie farmland near Drumheller.** *Bottom*: **Lake Athabasca at Fort Chipewyan, Alberta's corner of the Canadian Shield**

above ground only in the northeastern corner. The towns of Fort Chipewyan and Fitzgerald are built on the Shield.

Water

Alberta's water supply comes from ice, surface water and ground water. Glaciers and the Rocky Mountain snowpack are the source of most of the rivers that flow through the province. The north and central parts of Alberta have a good supply of surface water. The southern portion does not. Although Alberta has 16 796 square kilometres (6483 square miles) of fresh water, there are only three large natural lakes: Lake Claire, Lesser Slave Lake and Bistcho Lake. In addition, about one-third of Lake Athabasca lies in Alberta. The rest is in Saskatchewan.

Big Island, Lake Bistcho, in the northwest corner of the province, is accessible only by air. *Inset:* **The North Saskatchewan River near Edmonton**

Each of Alberta's three main watersheds drains into a different body of salt water. The Peace, Hay and Athabasca river systems flow into the Arctic Ocean through the Mackenzie River. The North and South Saskatchewan rivers drain eastward into Lake Winnipeg, then through the Nelson River into Hudson Bay. The Milk River carries water from the southern tip of Alberta into the Missouri River which joins the Mississippi and empties into the Gulf of Mexico. Some Alberta rivers have been dammed to provide city water supplies, water for irrigation and electric power.

Underground streams, or aquifers, and fresh-water springs provide water for industry, irrigation, home and farm use. Hot springs in the mountains near Banff and Jasper attract thousands of visitors each year.

Climate

Alberta, in the cool temperate zone, has a four-season, changeable climate. It is so changeable near the mountains, that people say: "If you don't like the weather, just wait five minutes."

The first frost-free day in spring usually occurs about May 10 in Medicine Hat and May 15 in Edmonton. Most years, the snow in the mountains melts in late May or early June, except on the higher peaks where it stays all year round.

The warmest months are July and August, with July being the hottest. Temperatures can rise to 32° C (90° F) and occasionally to over 38° C (100° F), but the humidity is low and evenings are cool, even in July.

Autumn is beautiful in Alberta. After the first frosts, Indian summer, a period of warm or mild weather, arrives. Although Indian summer nights can be cold, the days are often as warm as those of July, making Albertans forget that snow is on the way.

For five or six months of each year, Albertans live with snow. The snow often comes in October or November and stays until March or April. Snowfall is greatest in the mountains. Although the prairies

Left: **Autumn in the Kananaskis region where mountain and prairie meet.**
Below left: **Winter in the Rockies — Peyto Lake, Banff National Park.**
Below: **Calgary postie in the snow**

have less snow, they do experience blizzards that sometimes kill humans and animals with their high windchill factor, a combination of low temperature and wind speed, and reduced visibility.

The coldest month is usually January. Winter temperatures can rise or fall quickly depending on the wind direction. If it blows from the north the temperature drops. If the wind is from the west, Albertans know they are about to get a break from the cold weather. An arch of clouds in the west signals the arrival of a chinook, a warm dry wind that can raise the temperature as much as twenty-five degrees Celsius (forty-five degrees Fahrenheit) in one hour. Within a few hours the ground can be bare of snow.

Alberta winters are marked by frequent temperature inversions, a layer of warm air sitting on top of a cold air mass. Inversions increase air pollution by trapping emissions from vehicles and industry near the ground. Edmonton and many other communities have several inversions every winter.

Plants and Animals

Most of Alberta is covered by three kinds of vegetation: grassland, parkland and boreal forest. The grasslands range from the short-grass prairie near Medicine Hat to the tall grasslands along the Porcupine Hills. From spring to late fall, wildflowers add a splash of colour to the grasslands. Furry crocus buds are first out of the

In spring and summer, carpets of colourful alpine flowers, such as fireweed, columbine, clematis and saxifrage brighten the often stark mountain landscapes.

ground in the spring. In May the yellow bean spreads a bright carpet over the greening landscape. Month by month — from June's yellow sunflowers to September's purple asters — wildflowers provide beauty for the human eye and food for animals such as the Richardson's ground squirrel. Pronghorn antelope, mule deer and coyotes are often seen grazing or hunting on the prairie. The many sloughs and potholes are nesting grounds for ducks, geese, swans and white pelicans.

Parklands, where grasses give way to aspen and alder trees and bushes such as saskatoon and chokecherry, are a transition zone between the plains and the boreal forest. Most plains animals, plus moose, wolf, black bear, fox and snowshoe hare make their home in the parklands. Hawks, owls, partridge, jays and grouse are common to plains, parklands and boreal forests.

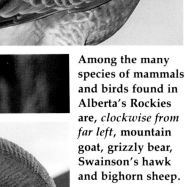

Among the many species of mammals and birds found in Alberta's Rockies are, *clockwise from far left*, mountain goat, grizzly bear, Swainson's hawk and bighorn sheep.

Alberta's boreal forest and some of its residents — bison, showshoe hare, elk and coyote

Alberta's boreal forests consist mainly of pine, spruce, Balsam fir and poplar trees. Birch, larch and willow are intermingled with the more prominent species. The boreal forest is home to all of Alberta's animals except the bighorn sheep, mountain goat and pronghorn. Moose, deer, woodland caribou, wood bison, snowshoe hare, fox, coyotes, wolves, weasels, beaver, hawks, owls, bald eagles, cougar, bobcat and lynx live in the forest.

Insects flourish in Alberta. Butterflies add flashes of colour to fields and woods. From June to September, flies, mosquitoes and

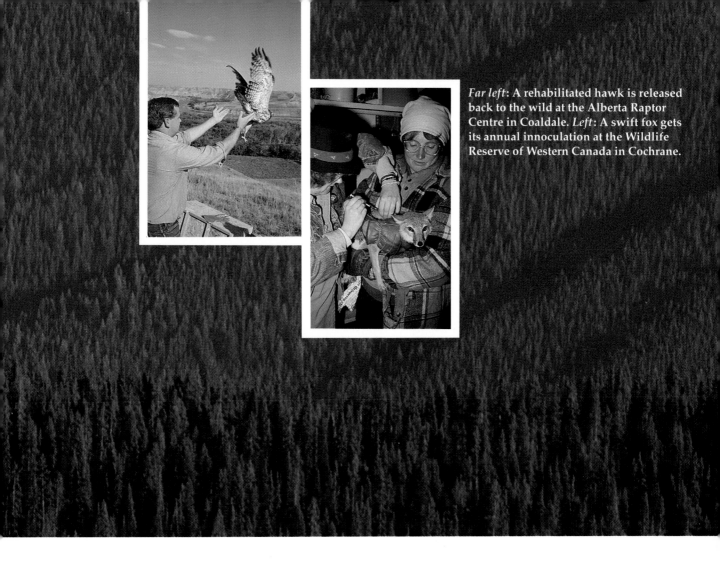

Far left: A rehabilitated hawk is released back to the wild at the Alberta Raptor Centre in Coaldale. *Left*: A swift fox gets its annual innoculation at the Wildlife Reserve of Western Canada in Cochrane.

hornets can make life miserable. Luckily, songbirds eat thousands of these insects per day.

Albertans are working to save some of the province's plants, birds and animals that are in danger of becoming extinct. A grizzly bear sanctuary has been set up at Swan Hills. The Calgary Zoo is raising whooping cranes as part of a program to re-introduce them into the wild. Farmers and the Alberta Fish and Game Association are helping burrowing owls make a comeback.

CHAPTER 3

The People

Far left, clockwise from bottom: Park Warden, Jasper National Park; Native woman braiding friend's hair before Calgary Stampede parade; South American refugee children performing at Saturday School in Calgary; Cowboy with red fiddle. *This page, clockwise from bottom*: Klondike Days in Edmonton; Branding cattle at Big Valley; Junior cowboys at a rodeo; Steel band at the Caribbean Festival in Calgary; School trip to Kerry Wood Nature Centre in Red Deer

21

Alberta's population reached just over 2.5 million in 1991, giving the province a population density of 3.8 persons per square kilometre (9.8 per square mile). Slightly less than 10 percent of Canada's population resides in Alberta. The province expects to keep growing for three reasons. The current economy is stronger than it is in other parts of Canada; the Canadian government is encouraging international immigration; and there has been a small natural population increase since 1988 of about 28 000 per year.

Many Albertans are moving to the city. Over 79 percent now live in urban areas. There are fifteen cities in Alberta with populations between 6000 and 700 000 or more. Calgary, with a population of 710 677 and Edmonton, with 616 741, are the two largest urban centres. Except for Grande Prairie and Fort McMurray, Alberta's cities are located near or south of Edmonton. Many Albertans live in towns and villages rather than cities or rural areas.

There were no cities or towns in what is now Alberta when Canada was born on July 1, 1867. For thousands of years Alberta's Native people had occupied the land. While they lived in small groups and temporary encampments, they hunted the huge herds of buffalo and other wildlife. In 1875, Alberta's two largest cities, Calgary and Edmonton, were just fledgling settlements around a police post and fur fort. Communities grew quickly at the end of the 1800s as settlers accepted Canada's offer of 65 hectares (160 acres) of free land. By 1906, one year after Alberta became a province, its population had grown to 185 412. It had more than doubled to 374 663 by 1911. There was very little growth during the First World War, but in the 1920s immigration increased. Many of the newcomers settled in the Peace River country. Population growth stalled again during the Second World War.

Above: Calgary, 1902. *Far left*: Calgary today. *Left*: One of the original Leduc oil rigs now stands in Calgary's Heritage Park as a monument to the 1947 oil discovery that marked the beginning of a spectacular growth period for the province.

It was not until 1947, when oil was discovered at Leduc, that Alberta had another growth spurt. For the next thirty years, unrest in Europe and Asia, plus changes and conflicts in Africa and South America prompted many people to seek a new life in Alberta. By the 1970s, Alberta had a population of over 2 million. The recession of the early 1980s caused the population to stay at 2.3 million from 1982 to 1986. It has grown slowly since then to just over 2.5 million in 1991.

Ethnic Mix

Alberta's multicultural society includes about 44 percent of British ancestry (including Americans of British origin), 11 percent German, 6 percent Ukrainian, 5 percent French, 4 percent Scandinavian, 3.2 percent Natives and 3 percent Dutch. People from just about every country in the world make up the other 23.8 percent.

The Native people of Alberta, who once dominated the land, now occupy only small parts of the province. In 1990, about 36 000 status Natives lived on ninety-one reserves and just over 19 400 lived off the reserves in towns and cities.

Recently, Alberta has been attracting more immigrants from Asia than from Europe. People from South and Central America are coming to Alberta as well. All newcomers are encouraged to keep their cultural heritage as they build new lifestyles.

People who share a culture are generally inclined to settle in the same area. Thus, from the early 1900s, Edmonton and its surrounding districts have had a large Ukrainian population. Albertans of

Native artist Gerald Tailfeathers juxtaposed the old and the new in his 1956 painting *Blood Camps*.

Japanese descent tend to live in the Lethbridge area. New Norway, Sundre and Grande Prairie have concentrations of Scandinavians.

While ethnic diversity brings challenges to tolerance and understanding, it also brings a cultural richness. Most Albertans are proud of their mixed cultural heritage and work at maintaining a peaceful and tolerant environment in the province. Albertans celebrate their colourful cultural background every August on Heritage Day.

Religion

The Native people had their own religion well before the West was open for settlement. Catholic priests and Methodist ministers came to Alberta in the fur-trading days to teach them Christianity. Missions and schools were already operating before the homesteaders arrived. Some settlers came to Alberta seeking the freedom to practise

Mormon picnic. Unlike the many settlers who lived on isolated homesteads, most Mormons lived in villages, farming the surrounding countryside. They were thus able to enjoy a more active social life than many of Alberta's early settlers.

Below: The Mormon Temple at Cardston, built of hand-shaped, white granite stone in 1911–23. *Bottom*: the Islamic Centre, Calgary. *Right*: St. Paul's Chapel at Fish Creek, built by the first Anglican missionaries in the Calgary area

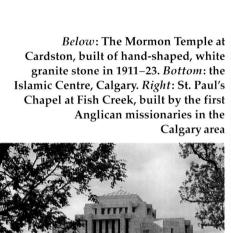

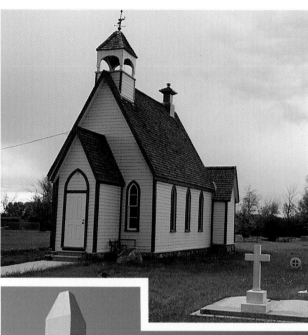

their religion. Mormons from Utah came to settle in southern Alberta because some of their customs were not accepted in the United States. Other groups, such as Hutterites and Mennonites left Europe because their religious beliefs clashed with the laws of their homelands. One of the first things many homesteading communities did was build a church and choose a minister or priest.

As new Albertans came from all over the world, they brought their religions with them. Islam, Judaism, Buddhism and many other religions are practised in Alberta. Some Natives worship in Catholic, Anglican, Mormon and Full Gospel churches, while others follow their traditional spiritual beliefs.

Holy Cross Roman Catholic Church at Fort Macleod

CHAPTER 4

Furs, Forts and Bibles

Long before Europeans came to North America, there were people living on the plains and in the northern forests of Alberta. The Blackfoot, Blood and the Peigan were members of the Blackfoot Confederacy and together with the Sarcee, lived on the plains. The Woodland Cree, Beaver, Chipewyan and Slavey inhabited the northern forests. Both the plains and northern Natives believed in a creator who guided their lives. All living things were treated with respect and dignity because all had a spirit. Mother Earth, thunder, wind, sun, moon and stars contributed to life. Both groups called on their spiritual oneness with all things through ceremonies, dance, music, songs, visions and dreams.

Northern Natives lived in groups of one or two families who travelled and worked together. *Nehiyawak* (nee hee' a wok) or Cree families were skilled at surviving in the forests. They knew the animals and how to hunt them. A hunter believed that a moose, deer or elk allowed itself to be killed so that he could feed his family. The Cree said a prayer and gave a gift of tobacco to ask forgiveness for taking plants and animals from Mother Earth. Cree women gathered plants for food and medicine, picked berries and trapped small animals. They skinned and tanned the hides of larger animals for clothing and moccasins.

To the Plains Indians, the buffalo was the most sacred member of the animal world. It provided their food, clothing and shelter. Even before they obtained horses and guns, plains Indians could kill

Overleaf: **Plains Indians hunting buffalo. After horses arrived on the Canadian plains in the mid 1700s, there was less need for the pounds used in earlier days. A large party of hunters could surround a herd and shoot several hundred of the animals as they ran.**

The skin-covered tipis of the Plains Indians could be put up in a few minutes —
a task usually performed by the women. *Inset*: Blood medicine woman

many buffalo at one time by driving them over a cliff or into a
pound. Before a buffalo hunt began, it was thought about and
planned. Songs and prayers asked the buffalo to let itself be killed
so that the people could live. When the hunt began, each person
knew his or her task and followed the plan. Women made pemmi-
can from dried buffalo, deer, moose or elk meat and dried berries
such as saskatoons, blueberries or cranberries.

The introduction of the horse made buffalo-hunting much easier.
The horse was to the Blackfoot what the tractor is to the prairie

farmer. It also replaced the dog for transporting homes and belongings between winter and summer camps. The Blackfoot became superb horsemen and the number of horses a man owned was a sign of his success. Horse-raiding was one way for a young man to prove his bravery. Unfortunately, it also led to feuds as individuals and bands got even for raids on their herds.

Fur Traders

Much of the early knowledge about western Canada and the beginnings of many Alberta settlements came from the fur trade. With the help of their Indian guides and wives, fur traders followed rivers and walked overland in their search for fur-bearing animals. They built forts and sent Europeans to trade with the Native North Americans. The Crees' hunting and trapping skills plus their nomadic lifestyle made them valuable partners in the fur trade. Cree hunters brought muskrat, otter, marten, fox, mink and beaver pelts to trade for blankets, copper kettles, steel knives, axes, guns and liquor. The quality of a hide, and hence its value, depended on the skill with which Cree women cleaned, stretched and dried the pelt.

Anthony Henday is believed to be the first European to have entered Alberta. He was sent by the Hudson's Bay Company in 1754 to ask the Blackfoot to bring furs to Hudson Bay. They refused. The Blackfoot Confederacy depended on the buffalo which tied them to life on the plains. Hudson Bay was too far away and plains people did not use canoes.

Peter Pond had better luck with the Cree in the Lake Athabasca area. In 1778, Pond crossed the portage between Methy Lake and the Clearwater River. Following the Clearwater, he came to the Athabasca River and then Lake Athabasca, where he built a trading post for the North West Company. The post, near present-day Fort Chipewyan, was used to collect furs from the Mackenzie River basin and the Peace River country.

Competition between the Hudson's Bay Company and the North

West Company resulted in the establishment of most of the forts in the area that eventually became Alberta. In 1795, Angus Shaw, a Nor'Wester, built Fort Augustus on the North Saskatchewan River. The same year, the Hudson's Bay Company built Edmonton House right beside it. Today, the city of Edmonton covers the sites of both forts.

The Hudson's Bay Company hired a surveyor named Philip Turnor to provide information about Rupert's Land, their fur-trading area. Turnor taught his surveying skills to company employees David Thompson and Peter Fidler. David Thompson and his wife Charlotte, a Native woman, travelled the North Saskatchewan and Athabasca rivers. On his final trip, Thompson recorded the existence of the Athabasca Pass. He produced the first accurate map of western Canada in 1813.

By 1821, competition for furs between the Hudson's Bay Company and the Nor'Westers was driving both companies into bankruptcy, bringing their Indian partners into battle and destroying

Métis encampment

the fur-bearing animals by over-trapping. Realizing this, the two companies decided to merge, keeping the name Hudson's Bay Company. Fewer animals were trapped now, the rum trade was reduced and inter-tribal wars were discouraged.

Although the plains people were not as involved in the fur trade as the northern groups, guns, horses and increased numbers of outsiders did change their lifestyle. As the fur trade spread further into the West, the Natives came to depend more and more on the traders and their goods. Smallpox, measles and tuberculosis emptied hundreds of tipis.

One happy result of the fur trade was a brand new people: the Métis. Scottish and French-Canadian fur traders married Indian women. Their children, the Métis, learned the skills and customs of both races. The Métis built some of the first communities in Alberta at Lac Ste Anne and St. Albert.

Missionaries

The first missionary to enter what is now Alberta, Reverend Robert Rundle, was a Wesleyan minister. He arrived at Fort Edmonton in

Fort Edmonton. Every spring a boat brigade laden with furs left Fort Edmonton for York Factory. Pointed barges, manned with 8 oars and using a square sail when the wind was fair, could carry 5 tonnes of cargo plus the crew of voyageurs.

1840. The first Catholic mission was established by Father Thibault in 1842. Ten years later he was replaced by Father Lacombe, who worked with the Cree and Métis at Lac Ste Anne and later at St. Albert. For many years, Father Lacombe was a peacemaker between the Cree and Blackfoot, and later he helped maintain peaceful relations between Natives, railway builders and settlers.

By 1863, Reverend George McDougall, his son John and their families were operating a Methodist mission northeast of Edmonton. Continued outbreaks of smallpox between 1869 and 1871 caused the McDougalls to close the mission. Using Edmonton as their base, the two missionaries travelled among the Native and European populations until 1875. Then they built a mission for the Blackfoot at Morley, west of Calgary.

Missionaries like the McDougalls and Father Lacombe came to care deeply for the Native peoples among whom they worked. They did their best to influence the government to deal with them in a more fair and understanding way.

CHAPTER 5

Buffalo Robes to Hard Hats

When the Dominion of Canada took ownership of the West in 1870, it was in a state of disorder. For several years the authority of the Hudson's Bay Company had been lessening. Free traders from the United States peddled whiskey and repeating rifles for fur pelts and bison hides. The buffalo herds on which the plains people depended were being slaughtered. Murder, stealing, drunkenness and brutality were increasing. By 1870, the Native population was demoralized by the disorder and a smallpox outbreak that had just killed an estimated 1200 to 1500 people.

This lawlessness led the Government of Canada to form the North-West Mounted Police (NWMP) especially to police the West.

Overleaf: **North-West Mounted Police escorting the Duke of Cornwall and York — later King George V — during a visit to Calgary in 1901.** *Below*: **When a huge rock slide crashed down on the town of Frank in 1903, Mounted Police led the rescue operations and turned their detachment building into an emergency hospital.**

The force reached Edmonton and Fort Macleod in 1874 and in the next few years built posts at Calgary and Fort Saskatchewan. Order was restored and a few people began to settle around the police posts. Métis settlers from Manitoba established communities at St. Albert, Lac Ste Anne, Lac La Biche and Buffalo Lake.

In the wake of the NWMP came government surveyors, marking out land for the railway and for farms, and a slowly increasing number of settlers. Wise native leaders like Crowfoot, Chief of the Blackfoot, watched as fences sprang up and the bison herds dwindled, and realized that the old way of life of the plains people was doomed.

Crowfoot, chief of the Blackfoot, declares his loyalty to Queen Victoria at the signing of Treaty No. 7, September 1877.

In 1876 and 1877 the Blackfoot, Cree, Stoneys and Sarcee signed treaties with the Canadian government, under which they gave up their right to most of the land in return for reserves set aside for their sole use, some cash benefits and help adapting to a new way of life.

By this time it was too late to save the buffalo, and the last herds disappeared from the Canadian plains during 1878 and 1879. There was hunger on the new reserves. The NWMP obtained some meat from Montana and the few ranches operating in southern Alberta, but it was not enough. Six hundred or more Blackfoot starved to death.

Life for northern natives continued much as it had during the fur trade days. Treaties were signed and reserves created for most northern bands in 1899.

When Indian and Métis discontent boiled to the surface in the North-West Rebellion of 1885, there was fear that the Blackfoot, Cree and Métis of Alberta would join the fighting. Louis Riel sent messengers to the Blackfoot chief, Crowfoot, to Red Crow of the Bloods and to the Métis at St. Albert asking for their help. Although they all decided to stay out of the conflict, two northern Cree bands under Big Bear and Poundmaker joined Riel.

Many settlers in the District of Alberta were terrified at the thought of an Indian and Métis uprising. At the Canadian government's request, Thomas Strange, a retired British army officer, took command of the district and organized the Alberta Field Force. Leaving the protection of southern Alberta to the Rocky Mountain Rangers, Strange and the Alberta Field Force set off through bush and muskeg to reinforce Edmonton and capture Big Bear's band. From Edmonton, part of the Field Force went down the North Saskatchewan River by boat while the rest marched to Frenchman's Butte where they fought a battle with Big Bear's warriors. Neither side won. Strange decided to wait for supplies and reinforcements and while he waited, the Cree vanished into the bush. After some weeks, Big Bear and Poundmaker turned themselves in to the

Black rancher John Ware and his family. Ware came to Alberta on a cattle drive, from Montana in 1882. After a few years of working for others, he established his own ranch on the Red Deer River and became widely known for his bronco-busting and steer-roping skills. Today, his log cabin can be seen in Dinosaur Provincial Park.

authorities. They were imprisoned and their spirits broken. Neither survived long. After the rebellion was put down, the rebels who had been captured or given themselves up were tried. The decision to hang Riel and eight Indians caused a continuing controversy in Canadian history.

Ranchers

The foothills and short-grass prairie of southern Alberta were ideal for ranching. The nutritious grass and warm chinook winds made it possible to graze cattle year round. Soon, the Canadian Pacific Railway would carry beef to eastern markets. In the meantime, the Natives, NWMP and the railway construction gangs all needed beef.

The Canadian government leased 40 000 hectares (100 000 acres) to ranchers for twenty-one years at 2.5 cents per hectare (1 cent per acre). Senator M.H. Cochrane was the first rancher to sign a lease. His land was in the Bow River valley west of Calgary where the town of Cochrane now stands. By 1885, 126 ranchers were grazing 75 000 cattle on 1 539 373 hectares (3 803 791 acres). In contrast to the "Wild West" image it held in the United States, ranching in Alberta resembled life on an English estate. Many of the ranchers were retired NWMP officers. Others were absentee owners who visited occasionally to inspect their cattle and admire the scenery. As the government encouraged more and more settlers to claim prairie land in the early 1900s, ranching declined. Many of the big ranches died just as Alberta was born.

The Railway

While Canadian Pacific Railway (CPR) workers built track westward, other people were getting the prairies ready for settlement. In the 1880s, land surveyors marked the prairie into 65-hectare (160-acre) squares. Scientists studied routes for railways and soils, and reported on coal and mineral wealth. When the CPR tracks reached Calgary in 1883, settlers and farm workers soon followed. The railway provided an efficient way of transporting beef and farm products to market. Extension of the tracks north made Edmonton a transportation centre for northern Alberta and later a jumping-off point for prospectors on their way to the Klondike seeking gold.

Between 1898 and 1914, nearly 600 000 American immigrants, mostly farmers from the midwestern states, came to the Canadian prairies. This group from Colorado settled at Gem in March 1914.

Settlers

Until about 1896, relatively few farmers had come to Alberta. The first settlers in the Calgary area were Jane and Sam Livingston. Several NWMP members settled near Calgary when they retired from the force. Most of Alberta's earliest settlers came from Ontario and Quebec to the parkland south of the North Saskatchewan River. In 1887, Mormons, led by Charles Ora Card, settled the dry southwest corner of Alberta. About the same time a group of Germans came to farm south and west of Edmonton. Demand for houses brought small sawmill operators into the foothill forests. Coal for heating homes had been available from Lethbridge since 1869 when Nicholas Sheran opened the first mine. The Galt family began shipping coal from their Lethbridge mine in 1885. With the help of government money, they built a railway from their mine to the CPR tracks. Miners moved in and Lethbridge prospered. In 1885, natural gas was discovered near Medicine Hat. By 1890 it was being used to heat homes and businesses.

Below: **The trek to the new homestead.**
Left: **The original log home of Charles Ora Card, leader of Alberta's first Mormon settlers, is now a museum.**

Clockwise from right: Women were often left in sole charge of the homestead when men had to seek paid work to earn the cash needed for equipment and supplies; for a long time Ukrainian immigrants built their houses with thatched roofs and whitewashed walls, just as they had in their homeland; Polish farmers of Tide Lake preparing for a Thanksgiving ceremony; when the CPR was finished, many Chinese workers opened laundries and/or restaurants in the towns that sprang up along the railway lines.

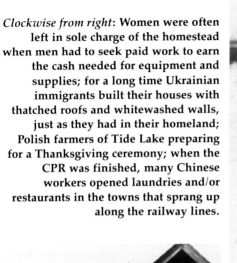

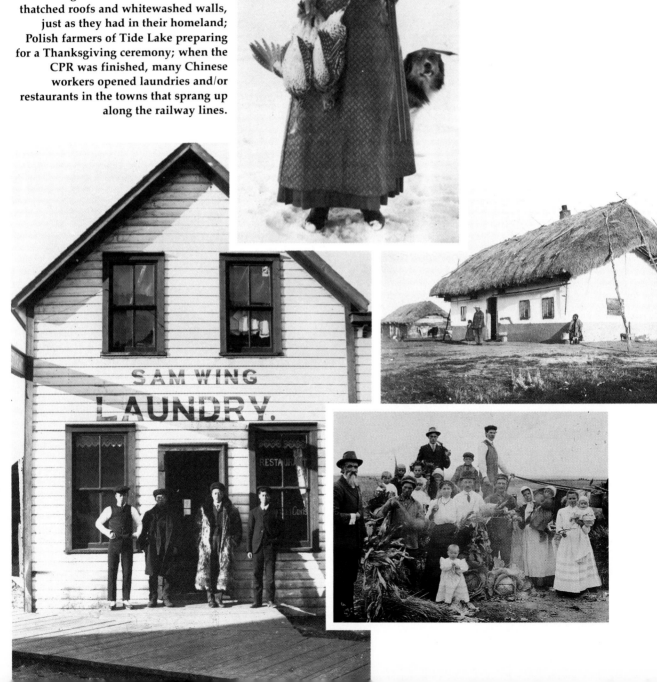

In 1896, Clifford Sifton was appointed Minister of the Interior by the Canadian government and made responsible for bringing settlers to the West. His job was made easier when the United States stopped selling land in the American West. Sifton advertised the wonderful life on free land that awaited any European or American who would come to western Canada. Come they did! Boat loads came from the Ukraine, Great Britain, France, Germany, Scandinavia and eastern Europe. Wagons full of farm families arrived from the United States.

Most of those who came staked their claim to a homestead and did their best to survive. Although some gave up and left, many

Almost every village had a general store that sold everything from hardware and hats to soap, socks and sugar. *Inset*: Blacksmith shop at Innisfail

withstood the mosquitoes, cold, rough shelter, prairie fires, hunger, loneliness, monotony and endless back-breaking work. Eventually machinery made life a little easier, and years later when the settlers paused and looked back, they saw grain fields all the way to the horizon. One generation of men and women had changed forest and prairie into farms and homes. And while they were at it, they had created a new province.

Immigration to Alberta dwindled during the First World War but settlement began to spread into the northern half of the province

Not all of the immigrants who came to Alberta were homesteaders. Many settled in the rapidly growing cities, and many — though by no means all — prospered.

again in the 1920s and 1930s. However, long before these home-steaders arrived, two men had sung the praises of Peace River farmland. "Twelve-Foot-Davis," who traded along the Peace, told everyone he met about the good black soil in Peace River country. James Cornwall better known as Peace River Jim was one of the area's best promoters. He knew the country well: he was a trader, a riverboat captain and its Member of the Legislative Assembly (MLA). As MLA, Cornwall campaigned for a railway and telegraph into the north. He got both, while roads into the area were still only trails through the bush and muskeg. The railway reached Peace River in 1912, Grande Prairie in 1916 and Fort McMurray in 1917. A road from Grande Prairie to Edmonton was built in 1928-29.

The four supply centres — Edmonton, Calgary, Lethbridge and Medicine Hat — prospered during the Roaring Twenties, but the Dirty Thirties were a different story. The Great Depression hurt Alberta agriculture. Wheat prices were so low farmers could not pay the freight charges to get their grain to market. Hail and drought damaged crops. Businesses closed and towns withered away. Before Alberta recovered from the Great Depression, Canadians were going overseas to fight in the Second World War.

"Riding the rails" during the Great Depression. The practice was illegal, and railway police made some effort to stop it, but there were simply too many hoboes and too few police.

Many Albertans joined the armed forces. Regiments such as the Calgary Highlanders, Lord Strathcona's Horse, the Princess Patricia Canadian Light Infantry and the 10th, 31st and 49th battalions fought with other Canadians in Europe. As in other countries, women ran the farms, worked in factories and took over many other jobs traditionally performed by men during the war years. Training bases for British and Canadian airmen were established in Alberta as well as elsewhere in Canada. Development in Edmonton, Peace River and Grande Prairie got a boost from the construction of the ALCAN highway to Alaska and the Canol pipeline from Norman Wells in the Northwest Territories to Whitehorse in the Yukon. Edmonton became the headquarters and supply centre for the pipeline and for American planes on their way to Alaska and Russia.

Boom and Bust Years

In February 1947, the discovery of oil at Leduc launched the oil boom. Seismographic crews crisscrossed the province recording underground formations. Woodbend, Redwater and Pembina oilfields were discovered and tapped. Instant towns sprang up at Fox Creek, Rainbow Lake, High Level and Zama Lake. The 1950s were the pipeline decade as oil was sent to eastern Canada and the United States. Road-building increased to meet the industry's need for efficient transportation. Paved highways became common and the trucking industry boomed. Alberta's economy shifted from agriculture to oil and gas. The Princess Province had found its wealth.

Once again immigrants came to Alberta from all over the world, including the Pacific Rim countries, Asia, South America and the Caribbean. Alberta's multicultural society continued to develop. Boom towns flashed into existence: Grande Cache grew around coal mining; Hinton around pulp and paper. Drillers in hard hats pushed the search for oil throughout the province. Construction workers pushed city skylines higher. Every year Alberta was growing bigger and more prosperous.

Many people felt the province could keep on growing forever. Others saw a need to care for the environment through conservation. Laws were passed to protect the soil, watersheds, wildlife and forests. The Heritage Fund was established to save part of each year's money from oil sales for the future.

The 1980s began with a party as Alberta celebrated its seventy-fifth birthday, but the party was soon followed by a recession. Companies trimmed their spending and laid off employees. In 1987, the Alberta government chose to encourage development of the forestry and tourism industries to lessen the impact of low oil prices on the economy. People around the world, Albertans included, were becoming more concerned about the environment. Environmental groups began asking for a voice in industrial development.

Leduc No. 1. The discovery of oil at Leduc in 1947 changed the economic life of Alberta. Bankrupt in the 1930s, the province would soon be one of Canada's wealthiest. *Inset*: Blowing gas to reduce pressure

CHAPTER 6

Government and the Economy

The region that is now Alberta was originally part of the fur-trading territory known as Rupert's Land, which was granted to the Hudson's Bay Company by King Charles II of England. In 1870, the Dominion of Canada purchased Rupert's Land and renamed it the North-West Territories. In 1882, the Territories were divided into postal districts, one of which was named Alberta at the request of the Marquis of Lorne. The Marquis was Canada's Governor General at the time, and his wife was Queen Victoria's daughter, Princess Louise Caroline Alberta. Lake Louise, in Banff National Park, is also named after the Princess. The postal districts became electoral districts in 1886 when each was given representation in the Canadian Parliament. Ottawa governed the Territories until 1888 when they were granted their own elected Legislative Assembly, which met in Regina.

Population in the districts grew, but the annual grants of money from Ottawa did not. Money was needed to develop resources, build roads and bridges, provide services and pay administration costs. People in the Territories began to demand the same rights and powers that Canadian provinces had enjoyed since Confederation in 1867. In 1900, a formal request for provincial status was sent to the Dominion government. The issue was discussed for two years and then refused. During the next three years, debate raged over separate schools, resource ownership and land control, while politicians, newspaper editors and citizens lobbied for provincial status. Giving in to growing pressure, the Canadian government finally created the provinces of Alberta and Saskatchewan in 1905.

Lake Louise, one of the most photographed mountain landscapes in the world. The lake owes its milky green colour to glacial sediment.

George Bulyea was chosen as Alberta's first Lieutenant-Governor. He chose Alexander Rutherford, a Liberal, to be premier until an election could be held. The Liberals won twenty-three of the twenty-five seats in the 1905 election and Rutherford remained premier. This overwhelming vote for one party was an indication of the pattern that most Alberta elections would follow.

Breaking with Tradition

Socialism gained votes in Alberta's 1921 election. Coal miners in Lethbridge, Crowsnest Pass and Drumheller banded together to demand better wages and improved working and living conditions. When their voices were ignored, they formed the Canadian Labour Party (CLP). Four CLP candidates were elected in Alberta. The farmers, too, formed a political party to force better marketing practices and lower freight rates. That year the United Farmers of Alberta (UFA) won thirty-eight of the sixty-one seats in the Legislature. Farmers pressured the UFA government to create a co-operative grain marketing system. Henry Wise Wood helped establish the Alberta Wheat Pool and became its president in 1923.

In 1932, some UFA members helped to form the Co-operative Commonwealth Federation (CCF) which was more socialist than the UFA. Other UFA members did not agree with the policies of the CCF. This weakened the UFA and helped the Social Credit party to win fifty-six of sixty-three seats in the 1935 election. William Aberhart, Social Credit leader, campaigned with the message that the way to control the economy and end the Depression was for the people, not the bankers, to control credit. For the next thirty-six years, Alberta elected a Social Credit government. Ernest Manning became premier in 1943, followed by Harry Strom in 1968. The Progressive Conservative Party under Peter Lougheed ended Social Credit rule in 1971. The Conservatives continued to govern Alberta into the 1990s, first under Don Getty, then after December 1992 under Ralph Klein.

A Bennett Buggy, oxcart style. It was more usual for farmers to hitch horses to the car they could no longer afford to run during the Great Depression of the 1930s. Regardless, the set-up was called a Bennett Buggy after Richard B. Bennett who was prime minister from 1930–1935. *Inset*: William "Bible Bill" Aberhart led his Social Credit party to victory in 1935 with promises of fair wages, fair prices and a monthly "social dividend" of $25. He remained premier until his death in 1943.

Women's Rights

Alberta also broke with tradition in the swiftness with which it acknowledged the right of women to participate in the political process. Although Manitoba and Saskatchewan beat it by a few weeks in passing legislation that enabled women to vote in provincial elections and hold political office, Alberta often led the way in improving women's rights and status.

In the 1917 Alberta elections, Louise McKinney and Roberta MacAdams became the first women elected to a Canadian legislature. In 1921, Irene Parlby became the second woman in Canada to hold a cabinet post. By this time, Alberta had already pioneered legislation that ensured married women a share of family property, and the province had appointed the first woman judge in the British Empire — Emily Murphy.

In the 1920s, the question arose of appointing a woman to the

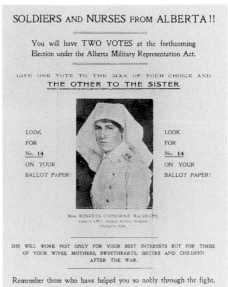

Left: When Alberta women won the vote on April 19, 1916, Nellie McClung, Alice Jamieson and Emily Murphy, three of the province's leading suffragists, celebrated by having their picture taken. *Right*: Roberta MacAdams won a seat in the 1917 election and so became one of the first two Canadian women to serve in a provincial legislature.

Canadian Senate. Objections were raised on the grounds that women were not "persons" under the law and could not therefore serve as Senators. It was five Alberta women — Emily Murphy, Nellie McClung, Louise McKinney, Irene Parlby and Henrietta Muir Edwards — who got together to challenge this ruling in the courts. When the Supreme Court of Canada ruled against them, they took their case to the Judicial Committee of the Imperial Privy Council in England (then the final court of appeal for Canada) and this time they won.

Federal Representation

Albertans live under a three-level system, in which federal, provincial and municipal governments each have specific responsibilities. Alberta had six seats in the Senate and twenty-six representatives in the House of Commons in Ottawa in 1993.

The imposing Alberta Legislature in Edmonton overlooks the North Saskatchewan River and is surrounded by elegantly landscaped grounds with terraces, fountains and pools.

Alberta has sent one prime minister to Ottawa — Joe Clark, who formed a short-lived (nine months) Conservative government in 1978. By then, Albertans had been voting overwhelmingly Conservative for twenty years, and they would continue to do so through the 1988 election. The 1993 election, however, produced a dramatic change: Albertans gave twenty-two seats to Preston Manning's Reform Party, four to the victorious Liberals and none to the Conservatives.

Under the Canadian constitution, Senators are not elected. They are appointed — officially by the Governor General, but chosen by the prime minister. There have long been calls for Senate reform, however, and in recent years in particular, many Albertans have campaigned for an elected Senate. In 1989, when an Alberta Senate seat was to be filled, Premier Don Getty put the question of who should fill it to a province-wide vote. Although the prime minister did not legally have to abide by the results, he later had the winner appointed to the vacant seat. Stanley Waters of the Reform Party thus became the first Canadian Senator elected by the voters of his province.

Provincial Government

The provincial government is formed by whoever has the backing of a majority of the elected members in the eighty-three-seat

Legislative Assembly. Usually this means the government is formed by the political party which elects the most members, but it could be formed by members of two or more parties who agree to work together to govern the province. The rest of the Members of the Legislative Assembly (MLAs) form the Opposition. Elections must be held every five years. The Lieutenant-Governor, who is the Queen's representative in Alberta, approves all laws. Lieutenant-Governors have no power to make or change laws because they are appointed, not elected. Alberta has an Ombudsman who considers the complaints of people who feel their rights have been violated.

The provincial government is responsible for the health, education, property and civil rights of all Albertans. It governs the use of natural resources, forests, electrical energy, highways and motor vehicles. Federal and provincial governments share responsibility for agriculture, immigration, trade, business, investments and labour relations.

Revenue and Expenditures (Spending)

The majority of the provincial government's money comes from coal, oil and gas royalties, taxes, fees and payments from the federal government.

Grande Prairie Regional College. The stunning buildings were designed by Alberta Métis architect Douglas Cardinal.

In the early 1990s, the provincial government adopted policies that are changing the way it does business. Such things as liquor stores and motor vehicle registration are being privatized. Government employees are being laid off as their jobs cease to exist. Major cuts in spending for health care and social services have been made. Public meetings are being held to reorganize social service programs and the health care system.

Municipal Government

The province is divided into local government districts, or municipalities, which elect council members to manage their affairs. Cities (some of which are municipalities on their own), towns and villages are run by an elected mayor and council. Although the federal government controls Indian reserves, many bands elect a chief and council to administer their affairs. The Elders advise the council and all band members meet regularly to share their ideas and concerns. Many band councils want the federal government to give them complete control of their communities. In Métis communities, the Métis local looks after municipal responsibilities.

Municipal governments obtain money from property taxes, fees, business taxes and provincial government grants. Some cities earn revenue because they own telephone, power and natural gas utilities. Provincial grants are used for education, recreation, recycling, tourism and cultural activites.

The Medicine Hat City Hall. The building, located on the banks of the South Saskatchewan River, won the Governor General's Award for Architectural Design in 1986.

The local government is responsible for public health, sanitation, utilities, transportation routes, fire safety and police protection. Municipal councils plan for houses, businesses and industries in their area. Native councils set up committees to direct jobs, health and education services.

Education

The first schools in Alberta were Roman Catholic and Methodist mission schools, founded in the 1850s. When Alberta became a province in 1905, one provincial system of education was established. Religious minorities were given the right and funds to operate separate schools in areas where the people requested them. Teachers were trained from 1906 in the Calgary Normal School, from 1912 in Camrose and from 1920 in Edmonton. The University of Alberta became responsible for teacher training in 1945.

Alberta has thirty-three post-secondary institutions, including five universities. The University of Alberta, established in 1908, is the oldest and largest in the province. The Universities of Calgary and Lethbridge opened in the 1960s to accommodate students in southern Alberta. Athabasca University offers home-study courses to students all over the province. The Banff Centre for Continuing Education teaches courses in the arts, in management and on the environment.

The Economy

For many years, Alberta's economy has been led by agriculture and energy resources such as oil, gas and coal, which depend on world prices. To lessen the impact of low prices for these goods, the government plans to broaden the economy. The forestry, petrochemical, food processing, high technology and tourist industries are being encouraged to expand.

Alberta exported goods to 145 countries in 1990. While the United

Left: Edmonton's first school. *Above*: Turn-of-the-century classroom in Horse Hills

Left: Students' Union Building, University of Alberta, Edmonton. *Above*: MacKimmie Library tower with a statue by George Norris, University of Calgary

States is Alberta's largest trading partner, Asia and the Pacific Rim countries are its fastest growing markets.

Agriculture

Over 30 percent of the province's land is used for agriculture. Grain, livestock, poultry, dairy products and vegetables are produced on 20 million hectares (50 million acres).

Top: Cowboys rounding up cattle near Pincher Creek. *Far right*: Canola field in the Peace River district, the most northerly farming area in Canada. *Right*: Southern Alberta wheat field

Wheat, canola and cattle are Alberta's major agricultural exports. In 1988, farmers harvested 5.3 million tonnes of wheat. Since then wheat production has remained high, but world prices have been low. Canola meal, canola oil and dehydrated alfalfa are processed in Alberta for export to Japan and the United States. Alberta produces about 44 percent of the beef used in Canada. Cattle and beef are also exported to Japan.

Farms are changing in Alberta. They are getting bigger and fewer in number. Large farms, we are told, can make more economical use of land and costly machinery. Farmers spent $500 million just on fuel and machinery repairs in 1988. Low prices for the traditional crops of wheat, barley and rye have brought about the introduction of new crops. Some farmers have begun growing field peas, beans, lentils, triticale, buckwheat and sunflowers.

Left: **Farm at High River in southwestern Alberta.** *Above*: **Irrigating fields near Lethbridge**

Oil and Gas

Abundant oil and gas resources have earned Alberta the title of the Energy Province. Alberta has three kinds of oil resources: crude oil, heavy oil and oil sands. Crude oil can be pumped out of the ground, but steam is needed to recover heavy oil. Oil sands, a mixture of sand, clay, water and bitumen, require inventive technology.

Alberta has two kinds of natural gas: sweet gas and sour gas. Sweet gas is the kind burned in household furnaces, while sour gas contains hydrogen sulfide. Refining sour gas yields sulfur, sweet gas and sulfur dioxide, a toxic waste gas. More than 600 Alberta gas plants process 450 million cubic metres (15.9 billion cubic feet) of raw gas per day. Thirty-eight percent of the refined gas is sold to California and other states, 34 percent to other parts of Canada and 28 percent is used in Alberta.

Albertans who know a lot about finding and producing oil and gas sell their knowledge and technology to other countries. Alberta companies, such as Safety Boss, helped Kuwait put out oil well fires caused by the Gulf War.

Manufacturing

For several years, manufacturing has been centred mostly in the oil, gas and agricultural industries. Now clothing, food products, furniture, forest products, chemicals, electronics, telecommunications and machinery are being produced. At present, the food and beverage industry is the largest manufacturing business. About half of the food processed is meat. This may change if a research centre set up near Leduc is successful in developing ethnic and gourmet foods.

The chemical industry produces methanol, ethylene and fertilizer. Chlorine and sodium compounds are manufactured for use in the pulp industry. Pulp and paper, lumber, plywood, chip boards and construction items such as doors and windows are manufactured in the forestry industry. Steel made from recycled scrap metal is used to manufacture oil and gas field equipment, agricultural machinery, forestry and construction products.

Clockwise from bottom: Limestone quarry; Petrocan Oil refinery in Edmonton; sulphur plant near Calgary; drilling for oil; garment worker. *Inset:* steel foundry

Forestry

Alberta's forestry industry is growing quickly since it became part of the government's plan to diversify the economy. Forests in which spruce, pine, fir, aspen and poplar are the main tree species cover about 55 percent of the province. Clear-cutting is the approved method for harvesting large amounts of timber in Alberta. Clear-cutting takes all the trees in two or more cuts, a few years apart, from one section of the cutting area. Trees must be replanted on the first cut and reach a certain height before the second cut of mature trees on the rest of the area can be made.

In 1990, fifty-four large sawmills produced over a million board feet of lumber. Sales of lumber, pulp, wood preservation products, poles and other wood products amounted to over $1 billion in 1990. Three-quarters of these products are sold out of the province. Lumber and pulp are exported to the United States and Pacific Rim countries. Residents of Grande Prairie, Hinton, Slave Lake, High Level, Whitecourt, High Prairie, Fox Creek and Athabasca work in the forestry industry.

Not everyone is happy about the rapid growth of the forest industry. Some people fear that decisions will be made too quickly

Patch-cut forest west of Calgary. Patch cutting is usually used for replanted forest. *Inset*: **Felling lodgepole pines by machine. The same machine is also used to gather the felled trees into bunches.**

before information from long-term research is available. People with ties to the natural forest do not want it to become a commercial forest. Some think logging roads may give the public too much access to the forest, causing damage from overuse. There is concern that more pulp-mill effluent will harm the Athabasca and Peace rivers. Now that forests are to be managed for profit, some people fear that herbicides will be used on grasses and poplar trees so that pine and spruce are "free to grow." This causes concern about the effects of herbicides on forest ecosystems, humans, wildlife and aquatic life. Forestry companies say new environmental legislation that changes the rules interferes with their long-term management of the forests.

Alberta forests have always had many different users. Forestry companies, oil and natural gas companies, miners, ranchers, trappers, campers and wildlife all use the forest. Some activities interfere with other uses. For example, oil and gas development interferes with timber harvesting and wildlife. Logging interferes with trapping. Pulp-mill effluent affects fish habitat. In the Weldwood forest-management area near Hinton, foresters and wildlife biologists are searching for ways to make different forest uses compatible.

Trade

Alberta maintains trade offices in New York, Los Angeles, London (England), Hong Kong, Tokyo and Seoul. The wholesale trade includes oil and gas products, food, machinery, farm products, lumber, building materials and motor vehicles, but the majority of trade workers are employed in the retail industry. Most retail sales take place in Alberta's urban centres. Edmonton's West Edmonton Mall, an internationally known centre, combines shopping, dining, recreation and entertainment.

Sales of automobile repair parts and accessories, food, drugs and household items amount to 73 percent of the retail trade. Clothing, furniture and appliances make up most of the other 27 percent.

Tourism

The tourist industry brought $2.6 billion to the Alberta economy in 1990, and provided employment equal to 75 000 full-time jobs. Almost half of the income from tourism came from Albertans themselves. Other Canadians provided 30 percent of the tourist revenue, the United States generated 16 percent and overseas visitors, 8 percent.

The Rocky Mountain scenery, Banff, Jasper and Waterton national parks, provincial parks and wilderness areas attract millions of visitors each year. Each year, as many as five million people will visit Banff National Park alone. Dinosaur Provincial Park near Brooks and Drumheller's Royal Tyrrell Museum of Palaeontology offer a feast of information and activities to dinosaur enthusiasts.

Below: The town of Banff in 1883, the year a CPR construction crew discovered the famous hot sulphur springs. Four years later, Banff National Park was created. It was Canada's first national park and is still the most popular. *Right*: Banff townsite today

Calgary and Edmonton are cosmopolitan cities with a variety of hotels, restaurants, shopping malls, parks and museums. A trip along the Forestry Trunk Road provides a close look at some of Alberta's natural mountain and forest areas.

Service Industries

The service industry includes many segments of the economy. Transportation, communication, wholesale and retail trade, finance, business, public administration, education, health care, accommodation, food, beverage and tourism all have a service industry component.

Many employees in this industry work with information. Government and businesses purchase engineering, architectural, legal, computer, accounting and employment information services. Four hundred firms in the province export computer services. Other companies export oil and natural gas engineering. In 1990, the sale of services generated more income for Alberta than the sale of goods.

Transportation

An excellent transportation system has evolved in Alberta. From canoe routes and Indian trails, a transportation network has grown that includes four- and six-lane paved highways, sections of two transcontinental railways, and two international airports.

Railways have been essential to the economic growth of Alberta. They provide transportation within the province and a link to sea ports. The Canadian Pacific Railway serves southern Alberta. The Canadian National operates in the central and northern parts of the province. The Alberta Resources Railway, built in 1969, transports coal, pulpwood, timber, oil and sulphur between Peace River country and Hinton. VIA Rail carries tourists and other passengers through the Rockies between Vancouver, Banff and Jasper.

The railway is indispensable to Alberta's role as the gateway to the north. Grain from Keg River and Fort Vermilion, ore from northern mines, lumber and crude oil are transported south by rail.

Above: Grain elevators at Champion, southeast of Calgary. *Right*: Highway near Lethbridge at dusk. *Inset*: A CPR train in Banff

A bush plane on a mercy mission to carry diphtheria vaccine to Fort Vermilion in 1929 stops for engine repairs at Peace River. The pilot, Wilfred "Wop" May, like most other bush pilots of the time, had flown fighter planes during the First World War.

Goods to supply communities in the Northwest Territories are shipped by rail and truck to the Mackenzie River where they are loaded on barges.

Alberta's highways have grown from "sunshine roads" (no sun, no road) to a 20 000-kilometre (12 400-mile) network of roads capable of carrying heavy traffic year round. Two national, east-west highways, the Trans-Canada and the Yellowhead, run through the province. Provincial highways 2 and 4 link Edmonton and Calgary with Montana. Highway 2 also connects Edmonton with the Mackenzie and Alaska highways.

Provincial bus routes provide freight, parcel and passenger service between cities and smaller communities. Many local, interprovincial and international trucking companies haul freight over Alberta roads. Exporters and importers have access to container-shipping facilities in both Edmonton and Calgary.

Air traffic has been important to Alberta since the 1920s when pilots such as Grant McConachie and Wop May carried mail and supplies to remote areas. As well, air service has been crucial in locating and developing resources in northern Alberta. Today, provincial airlines provide local and overseas business and tourist travel, airmail and container freight service.

Alberta's two international airports are located near Edmonton and Calgary. Air Canada and Canadian Airlines International fly from both airports across Canada, to the United States and Europe. Seven foreign-owned airlines provide direct flights to England, Germany, Italy, the Netherlands, Mexico, Asia and Australia.

Communication

The first newspaper published in Alberta was *The Edmonton Bulletin*. Frank Oliver began publishing the *Bulletin* in 1880. Its editorials sparked debate about the creation of Alberta and which city should be its capital. The *Bulletin* continued publishing until 1950 when it was sold to *The Edmonton Journal*. Today there are nine daily and 150 weekly newspapers published in the province.

Two daily papers are published in each of Edmonton and Calgary. *The Globe and Mail* arrives from Toronto via satellite and is then printed in the province. Red Deer, Lethbridge, Medicine Hat and Grande Prairie produce daily newspapers.

Weekly newspapers are published in French, English, German, Italian and Ukrainian. *Alberta Report*, a newsmagazine in English, is published weekly. Much of the news in weekly papers is sent in by the readers. Some papers have regular columnists, like Noreen Olson, whose entertaining wisdom appears in *At the Kitchen Table*, in *The Didsbury Review*. In the large cities, community papers publish the neighbourhood news.

Newspapers were the first owners of radio stations in Alberta. CJCA in Edmonton and CFAC in Calgary began broadcasting in May 1922. In the same year, W.W. Grant, who manufactured and sold radios, opened CFCN. Albertans tuned in to hear world

The Herald.

VOL I.   CALGARY, ALBERTA, JULY 2, 1885.   No. 1.

TELEGRAPHIC.

FORT PITT.

STRAUBENZIE, June 29.— It was intended to make the start for home immediately on the arrival of Gen. Strange's column, but the programme has been altered, owing to two companies of the 65th (Montpany of the ing been left Calgary and is are now ws, and on h left this move will be arms, which

The start the Royal the 9th and

TORONTO.

TORONTO, July 1.—The investigation into the charges against Warden Massie, of the Central Prison, will be held on Thursday. Nicholas Murphy will represent the Catholic convention in reference to the charges preferred against Massie of ili-treating the Catholic prisoners.

HALIFAX.

HALIFAX, July 1.—The Scott Act has been carried in Gainsboro County. Only twenty Anti-Scott Act votes were polled.

NEW YORK.

NEW YORK, June 30.—Mrs. Dudley's trial, on the charge of attempting to shoot O'Donovan Rossa, has commenced. The New York Irish are exhibiting great interest in the result.

STALLION.

A French-Canadian Stallion will stand for mares at Bain Bros Livery Stable. $10 per service. Calgary, June 28.

WANTED.

A situation as cook for surveying, mining or ranche company. Apply to C. K. Mason, at Ambrose Shaw's, gunsmith, Atlantic avenue, opposite the depot, Calgary.

Stray Horses.

Two mares. One brown, branded B D on left shoulder; 1 chestnut, branded C on left thigh.

Have been taken up on the Little Bow. Parties are requested to prove property, pay expenses, and take away. Apply to the North-West Cattle Company.

High River, June 28

Should this Meet the Eye

Of anyone who has met with a person of the name of George Derry (an Englishman) who took up land at Pine Creek, about 12 miles from Calgary, and who left that place in May, 1884, to go to the

Above: The *Herald*, Calgary's first newspaper, began publication in 1885. *Left*: Setting type by hand at Heritage Park Historical Village, Calgary

events, sports, music and religious programs. Farm families felt less isolated with "radio waves" linking them to the rest of Alberta and the world. Many people wrote to religious programs asking for prayers for relatives and friends who were ill. Others sent greetings and messages about where birthday presents might be hidden.

Now there are 174 local and Canadian Broadcasting Corporation (CBC) radio stations. Listeners use the radio as an alarm clock, a jogging companion or company while driving a car, truck or tractor, as a source of entertainment and world, community and traffic

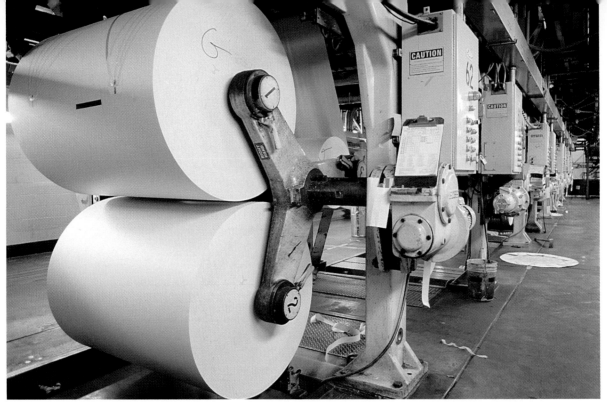

Loaded bales of newsprint in the pressroom of the *Calgary Herald*, Calgary

news. Today people phone in to request musical selections, or to enter contests and opinion polls.

Television came to Alberta in the 1950s offering mostly American programs. Today there are 118 television broadcasting stations in the province offering both Canadian and American programs. Provincial stations and the CBC provide music, drama and news. Some towns broadcast news, coming events and historical information on a community channel once or twice a week. The government owned ACCESS corporation produces and broadcasts educational programs to smaller communities via television. Major centres are connected by cable to American networks and satellites.

Alberta Government Telephones, which was established in 1908, has become one of Canada's largest telecommunication systems. In 1990, the Alberta government sold Alberta Government Telephones

Left: *Calgary Herald* **newspaper staff.**
Below: **Dave Maller of CFAC Radio, Calgary**

to private citizens. Now called AGT, it provides one of the most advanced mobile cellular telephone networks in North America. This network was developed partly to meet the demands for service from the oil and gas industry. AGT sells telecommunications engineering and management expertise around the world.

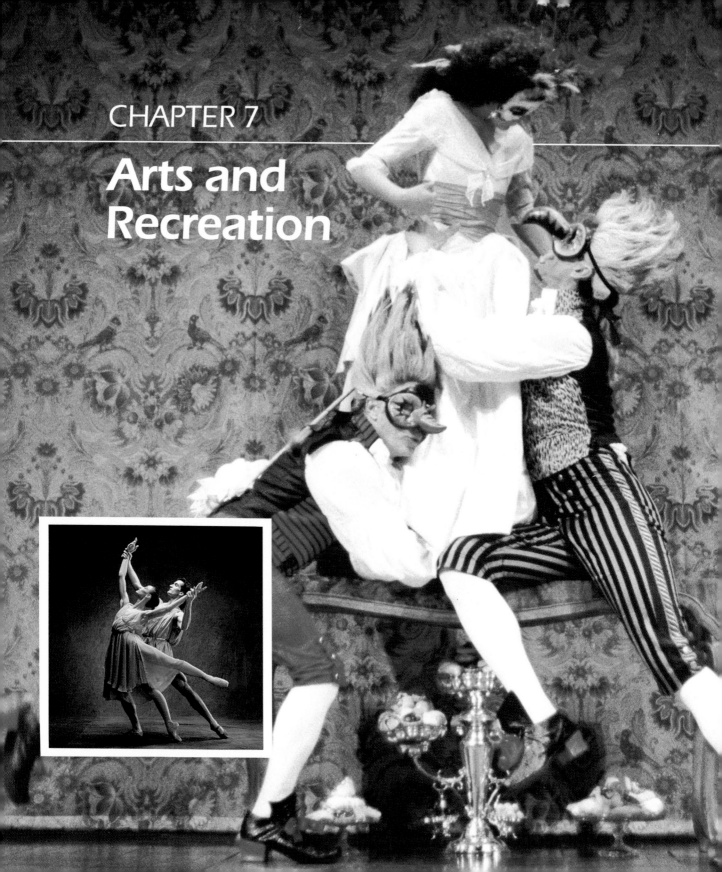

CHAPTER 7

Arts and Recreation

A rich and varied fare awaits visitors to Alberta's performing arts scene. There is everything from foot-stompin', hand-clappin', street dancin' to the Alberta Ballet Company's performance of *Swan Lake*. Alberta's larger cities have theatre and opera companies, philharmonic symphony orchestras, choirs, bands and dance troupes.

Theatre-goers can enjoy both professional and amateur performances in most cities and towns. Hollywood and television actors perform in dinner-theatre productions in the larger urban centres. Edmonton's Citadel Theatre presents performances worthy of any stage in the world. Community theatre groups, such as Sundre's Peak Theatre Players, consistently win provincial awards.

Many Alberta schools and universities have excellent drama programs. Betty Mitchell in Calgary established drama programs in the education system and started a drama group which evolved into Theatre Calgary. Professional mime and drama groups, such as The Tricksters, involve school students in drama productions and fine arts weeks. Performances at the Banff Festival of the Arts, held during July and August, develop from topics studied by artists at the Banff Centre for the Arts. Edmonton's Fringe, presented each August, is the biggest celebration of drama events in North America.

Alberta is movie country. The spectacular scenery has drawn film companies from eastern Canada, the United States, Japan and other countries to make movies here. Albertans have also made their mark in the industry, with two of the best-known names being

Theatre Calgary's performance of *Amadeus*. *Inset*: Soloists of the Alberta Ballet Company

75

A Calgary Opera production of the Christmas opera, *Amahl and the Night Visitors*

those of film maker Anne Wheeler (*Bye Bye Blues*) and actress Tan-too Cardinal, who appeared in the film *Dances With Wolves*. Young would-be film makers can train at the National Screen Institute in Edmonton.

Several performers, composers and conductors of classical, popu-lar and western music call Alberta home. One well-known musician, Tommy Banks, has worked with hundreds of stars, con-ducted symphony orchestras across Canada, and received a Juno award for the best jazz release. He has also composed and arranged musical scores for movies. Western singers Wilf Carter, k.d. lang, Ian Tyson and George Fox are all Albertans.

The province has many excellent adult, youth and children's choirs, such as the Calgary Boy's Choir, which has performed in Canada, the United States and Europe. Numerous ethnic choirs and dance troupes help keep cultural heritages alive while entertaining Albertan, Canadian and international audiences. Many bands, dancers and singers perform in parades and grandstand shows for celebrations such as Edmonton's Klondike Days, or Lethbridge's

Folk dancing demonstrations are a popular attraction at Calgary's Heritage Park.

Whoop-up Days. The Princess Patricia Canadian Light Infantry band, school, club and police bands march in parades in Alberta and other provinces. The Calgary Stampede Band has toured in Japan and other parts of the world.

Museums

Although Alberta is a young province, museums such as the Galt, the Glenbow and the Provincial house historical records and many fascinating artifacts. The Galt Museum preserves the history of coal mining in Lethbridge and of pioneering in general in southern Alberta. The Glenbow in Calgary has outstanding permanent collections of native and pioneer culture. Its educational program includes museum visits, activities and the loan of artifact kits. The Provincial Museum in Edmonton, which displays the natural and human history of the province, has programs similar to the Glenbow's. There are other museums featuring natural history, science and the province's history.

Most smaller communities have formed Historical Societies to preserve their histories and artifacts. Some community museums are built on land donated by an early pioneer and a town's original church or school sometimes becomes the museum, usually staffed partly by volunteers and students. Often there are demonstrations of the machinery or skills from the early years.

Alberta's historical parks exhibit native culture, NWMP posts, forts, and pioneer towns. Fort Macleod, site of the first North-West Mounted Police fort in the province, now has a replica of the original post. Early town buildings dating from 1900-1910 can be seen there as well. Fort Edmonton depicts a fur-trading fort as it might have been in 1846. In Fort Edmonton Park, there are historical villages representing Edmonton in 1885, 1905 and 1920. Visitors can ride on an antique streetcar and a steam locomotive.

Heritage Park in Calgary is a pioneer town museum composed of buildings moved to the site from settlements in southern Alberta. The bakery, hotel, general store and blacksmith shop operate as they did a century ago. Visitors may ride on a steam train, horse-drawn wagon or paddle-wheel boat. Sometimes guests are treated to a performance in the Canmore Opera House.

For over 6000 years, Plains Indians stampeded buffalo over the cliff at Head-Smashed-In Buffalo Jump. The Interpretive Centre (*below*) at the site provides fascinating insights into their vanished way of life.

Head-Smashed-In Buffalo Jump Interpretive Centre is built on one of the oldest, largest and best-preserved buffalo jump sites in North America. A buffalo jump is a high area over which buffalo were stampeded by Indian hunters. Head-Smashed-In was chosen to be a World Heritage Site in 1981. The centre blends into the Porcupine Hills so skilfully that it is visible only at close range. The architect, Robert LeBond, was given an award for its design. Head-Smashed-In is built on five levels, depicting the plains environment, the lifestyle of the Plains people, the use of the buffalo jump, the

Clockwise from bottom: Dinosaur Provincial Park where scientists have discovered some 35 species of dinosaurs; dinosaur skeleton at the Royal Tyrrell Museum of Palaeontology at Drumheller; a vintage vehicle parked in front of turn-of-the-century buildings, Heritage Park Historical Village, Calgary; Fort Macleod Museum depicts life as it was in the North-West Mounted Police forts.

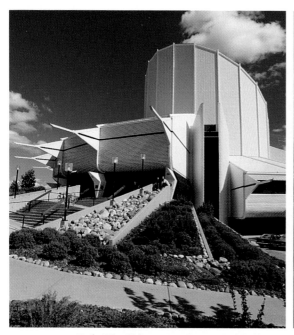

Left: **The Edmonton Space and Sciences Centre contains an IMAX theatre, planetarium and laser light show arena.** *Right*: **Calgary Centennial Planetarium with its special-effect star shows, observatory and hands-on exhibits**

effect of the horse, gun and European trade goods on the native life-style, and the archaeological program at Head-Smashed-In.

The Royal Tyrrell Museum of Palaeontology at Drumheller is Alberta's largest natural history museum. The Dinosaur Trail, a forty-eight-kilometre (thirty-mile) circle drive through the Red Deer River badlands, is the site of the fossil beds that led to the construction of the museum. Tyrrell displays include fossils, hands-on exhibits and one of the largest collections of dinosaur skeletons in the world. One hundred and forty kilometres (87 miles) southeast of Drumheller is Dinosaur Provincial Park. Thirty museums throughout the world display fossils from Dinosaur Park, a UNESCO World Heritage Site.

Edmonton's Space and Science Centre is the largest planetarium in Canada. It features an observatory, theatres and science exhibits. The Alberta Science Centre and Planetarium in Calgary presents special-effect star shows and hands-on science displays.

Libraries

Alberta's larger cities usually have a main library with several neighbourhood branches. Edmonton has twelve branch libraries plus the main Centennial Library located downtown in Sir Winston Churchill Square. The Edmonton system has a collection of 1.5 million items. Talking books are available for people who cannot cope with ordinary books and bookmobiles take the library to new residential areas. As part of the shut-in service, volunteers take books to homes of elderly, ill or handicapped people, to nursing homes and auxiliary hospitals. Edmonton's system has the second-largest circulation of library materials in Canada.

Libraries in smaller centres are part of a regional library system that gives them access to additional resources, expertise and services. Most libraries supplement their collections through inter-library loans.

Artists and Writers

Albertans have done a remarkable job of portraying their province and people to the world with pen, brush and camera. Paul Kane and perhaps a NWMP constable or two were the first artists to record life in this part of Canada. H.G. Glyde, who was a teacher of art as well as an artist, painted the working people of Alberta. His realistic paintings are a documentary of the urban and rural life of the 1920s and 1930s. Max Bates' paintings were just the opposite. Bates pioneered abstract painting in the late 1920s and later brought lithographic techniques to western Canada. Illingworth Kerr influenced Alberta art through his position as head of the Alberta College of Art from 1947 to 1967. His work helped make the College known and respected across Canada. Alex Janvier, who is known for his brilliantly coloured symbolic paintings, produced the mural for the Indians of Canada pavilion at Expo '67 in Montreal, Quebec. A.C. Leyton, acknowledged at the 1939 World's Fair in New York

Alberta art (*clockwise from top left*): A colourful mural decorates the exterior of the Ponoka Public Library; *Qu'Appelle River, Autumn*, by Illingworth Kerr; *The Lunchbreak*, a bronze sculpture by Seward Johnson, in Edmonton, is part of the Main Street Alberta program set up to beautify cities and towns across the province; Harry O'Hanlon's *The Family of Horses*, life-size bronze statues on the steps of the new City Hall, Calgary; *The Exodus* (1941) by H.G. Glyde

as among the world's finest water-colour artists, painted locomotives, gardens, totem poles, ships and landscapes. Paintings by Alberta artists have been purchased by the Alberta government as gifts for foreign visitors. Isobel Levesque is one of these artists. Her paintings capture the mood and seasons of the Alberta landscape.

Among writers, Andy Russell, James Gray, and Grant MacEwan have all spoken out for Alberta's land and lifestyle. More recently, Andy Russell has fought against the damming of the Oldman River. He is well known for his many books, including *The Rockies* and *Tales of a Wilderness Wanderer*. James Gray and Grant MacEwan have written extensively on the province's early history. Maria Campbell showed Albertans the pain and pride of being Métis. Jan Hudson's book, *Sweetgrass*, tells of a fifteen-year-old Blood Indian girl who lived in Alberta in the 1830s. William Kurelek wrote and illustrated books about life on a homestead from a boy's point of view. His paintings also bring to life the Canadian classic *Who Has Seen the Wind?* The poems, short stories and novels of Robert Kroetsch, Rudy Wiebe and Bill Kinsella document Alberta's multicultural identity. Jan Truss with books such as *Bird at the Window* and Marilyn Halvorson with *Cowboys Don't Cry* are authors with much to say about how young people cope with life and death. But Alberta's authors are not bound by time and space. Pauline Gedge took us back to Ancient Egypt in *Child of the Morning*, and Monica Hughes took us into the future with books such as her *Isis* trilogy.

Recreation

There is no need to be a couch potato in Alberta! Every season has opportunities for team sports, individual or group activities. The eleventh Commonwealth Games in 1978 and the 1988 Winter Olympics gave Edmonton and Calgary excellent summer and winter sports facilities. Edmonton has pools, indoor tennis, racketball and squash courts, a jogging track, weight rooms and a gymnasium for public use. In Calgary, a speed-skating oval, luge, bobsled and ski runs are available for both the novice and the professional. As well as these, there are a variety of winter activities for people who like snow. Skiing is ideal on the high slopes of the Rockies. Cross-country ski trails wind around city parks and through remote mountain valleys. Snowmobilers travel forestry roads and cutlines.

Biathlon competitors practise at the Canmore or Bearberry nordic centres. Community hockey teams book ice time on indoor rinks. Scrub teams play on outdoor rinks in parks and backyards. Hockey fans watch the rival Edmonton Oilers and Calgary Flames play at the Saddledome in Calgary or in the Northlands Coliseum in Edmonton. Gymnasiums and other indoor facilities are in demand for volleyball, racketball and squash by those who like their sports without snow.

Albertans have won fame on the ski hills and ice rinks. Ken Read and Karen Percy are championship skiers, and in 1992, Karrin Lee-Gartner brought Olympic gold in the women's downhill home to Calgary; Kurt Browning, four-time World Champion figure skater, is the pride of Caroline, Alberta — and the rest of the province. There are many famous Oiler and Flames hockey players. Wayne Gretzky was the most admired player in the eyes of young hockey hopefuls and their parents when he played with the Oilers. Before

Possibly the most successful team in Canadian sports history, the Edmonton Grads (*right in 1923*), won 502 of the 522 basketball games they played. Better known today are the Edmonton Oilers and the Calgary Flames (*below right*) and the Edmonton Eskimos and the Calgary Stampeders (*below*).

he retired from the Flames, Lanny MacDonald was a favourite with Calgary fans. Handicapped kids love him for his help with the Special Olympics.

When the snow melts, Albertans go hiking, mountain-climbing, back-packing, picnicking and trail-riding. Fishing and boating are enjoyed on many Alberta lakes and rivers. Summer is baseball and soccer time in the stadiums and community parks. Swimming, windsurfing, enjoying wave pools and water slides are popular summer activities. Albertans have excelled in sports other than winter ones. For example, Carolyn Waldo and Michelle Cameron won Olympic gold medals for synchronized swimming.

When the days grow cooler, football fans cheer on their chosen teams. The rivalry is as strong between the Calgary Stampeders and Edmonton Eskimos as it is between the Oilers and Flames.

Below left: **The Nakiska Ski Area at Mount Allen was the site of the 1988 Winter Olympics alpine ski events.** *Below right*: **Mountain biker at Lake Louise.** *Inset*: **Kurt Browning**

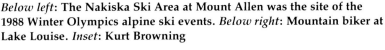

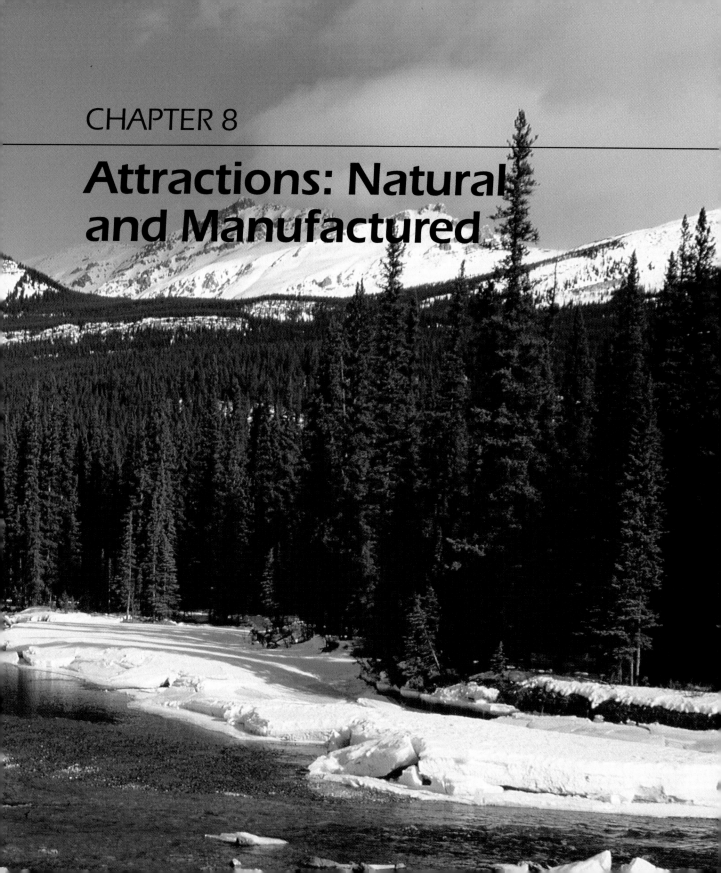

CHAPTER 8

Attractions: Natural and Manufactured

What is so great about Alberta? Variety. The natural scenery of prairie, forest and mountain is spectacular. The manufactured attractions include everything from Wild West shows to cosmopolitan cities; mammoth shopping malls to serene Japanese gardens.

To talk about the attractions in Alberta, it might be best to divide the province into three sections. The southern section would extend from the southern border to Red Deer. The central section would be from Red Deer to Edmonton. The northern from Edmonton to the border with the Northwest Territories.

In the southern section, two lovely natural areas are Waterton National Park and the Cypress Hills Provincial Park. Waterton and its American neighbour, Glacier National Park, joined in 1932 to become the world's first International Peace Park. The park offers mountain scenery, waterfalls and all the water sports associated with a long, still mountain lake.

There is a lake in Cypress Hills park, too, but the terrain is very different. The hills form a plateau that rises 1462 metres (4800 feet) above the prairie and was not covered by the ice sheet that ground across the rest of Alberta. Moose, deer, wild turkey, about 200 kinds of birds and 14 species of orchid are found in the park.

The cities of Medicine Hat and Lethbridge are in this area. Medicine Hat is built along the South Saskatchewan River on top of a natural gas field that was discovered in 1883 by a CPR crew drilling for water. This city of almost 44 000 people is located in the driest

Overleaf: **Castle Mountain. According to Indian legend, the summit is the home of the chinook — a warm winter wind that blows out of the Rockies and melts snow in the foothills and prairies.**

Mule deer at home in Waterton Lakes National Park, which is known for its U-shaped valleys, hanging valleys and canyons. *Inset*: A winter windstorm howls through the park.

part of the prairies. For many years Medicine Hat was famous for its pottery, produced from local clay deposits.

Lethbridge, with an area of 124 square kilometres (48 square miles), is located on the Oldman River. Also on the Oldman and just west of the city is the Blood Indian Reserve. The University of Lethbridge, a unique structure suited to the windy prairies, is built into the banks of the Oldman. In 1967, the Nikka Yuko Centennial Japanese Gardens were created in the city as a sign of friendship between Japan and Canada. The fur-trading and coal-mining history of the area is told at Fort Whoop-up and the Galt Museum.

Farmers around Lethbridge use irrigation to grow sugar beets, lentils, mustard, birdseed and vegetables. Nearby Taber is noted for its delicious corn. Backyard barbecues as far north as Red Deer are heated up for a corn roast when the truck from Taber pulls into town.

Fort Macleod and Head-Smashed-In Buffalo Jump are located between Lethbridge and the largest city in southern Alberta: Calgary.

The Olympic Plaza in Calgary with the old and new city halls in the background. *Inset*: the 190-m (623-ft.) Calgary Tower offers an amazing view of the city and surrounding areas. During the 1988 Olympic Games, the Olympic flame burned brightly from its top.

At an elevation of 1048 metres (3,440 feet), covering an area of 528 square kilometres (204 square miles), Calgary is built where the Bow and Elbow rivers meet. Downtown Calgary is on the south side of the Bow River. From the north, Centre Street leads over a bridge guarded by sandstone lions, through Chinatown to the foot of the Calgary Tower. The revolving restaurant at the top of the tower is an excellent place to view the city, mountains and prairie as 747s pass by on their way to the international airport.

Calgarians take their visitors to Heritage Park, Fort Calgary, the Calgary Zoo, the Glenbow Museum, Devonian Gardens, the Planetarium, the Energeum, the Saddledome and, of course, the Stampede. The Olympic Hall of Fame at Calgary Olympic Park is a spot Calgarians show with pride because so many of them were volunteers at the 1988 Games. Just outside the city are Calaway Park and Spruce Meadows. Calaway is a miniature Disneyland, and Spruce Meadows, one of the horse world's finest show-jumping facilities, attracts local and international competitors and visitors.

The Calgary Stampede has something for everyone including a parade, street dances, pancake breakfasts, hot air balloon races and rodeo events.

A Calgary sightseeing tour includes (*clockwise from below*): a bronze statue of a bronco-busting cowboy, Caribbean dancing, a reconstructed Indian village and the Saddledome, which has the world's largest free-span concrete roof.

The gates to Banff National Park are an hour's drive west of Calgary along the Trans-Canada Highway. A gondola ride up Sulphur Mountain to the highest tea house in the Rockies is a great way to enjoy the mountain scenery, although some people think that nothing can top the view from Chateau Lake Louise. Photographers snap pictures of alpine flowers, animals and mountains reflected in still green lakes. Active visitors may choose to golf, boat, fish, hike, bike, canoe, ski or soak in the Upper Hot Springs. The Banff Springs Hotel, which is the nearest thing Alberta has to a castle, plus the

The château-like Banff Springs Hotel, built in 1888 by the CPR. *Above*: Chateau Lake Louise stands on top of a glacial moraine that dams the lake.

Banff Centre School of Fine Arts, Luxton Museum and the annual Television Film Festival are a sample of the attractions Banff offers.

Dinosaur territory and Rocky Mountain House National Historic Park are also found in this southern section. Rocky Mountain House's importance as a fur-trading fort is shown in the park. In the Rocky area, white-water canoeing on the South Saskatchewan and Clearwater rivers is a thrilling experience. Every summer hundreds of sun lovers swoosh down the water slide, swim or sail, at Sylvan Lake. Tourists visit Ram River Falls, the Raven Fish Hatchery and the Bighorn Dam hydro-electric generating station.

In dinosaur territory along the Red Deer River between Brooks and Drumheller, climbing around the eroded cliffs and hoodoos is as interesting as viewing the Tyrrell Museum's dinosaur skeletons.

The bizarre and eerie landscape of the Red Deer Badlands was created by thousands of years of wind and water eroding the sandstone.

Drumheller is in the coal mining district of the Red Deer River badlands. The ghost towns surrounding Drumheller were once busy communities full of coal miners and their families. Now the families have moved away and the coal mines have become museums.

Red Deer, in central Alberta and home to almost 60 000 people, is famous for its International Air Show held each August. One of its better-known residents is Kerry Wood, an author and naturalist. Wood helped establish the Gaetz Lakes Sanctuary for migratory birds in 1924. His books describe his experiences with, and observations of, animals in his corner of Alberta.

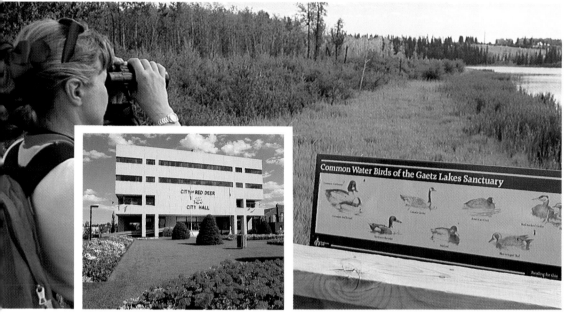

The Gaetz Lakes Sanctuary, just outside Red Deer, attracts more than 125 species of birds — and many birdwatchers. *Inset*: The Red Deer City Hall is situated in a large park containing some 40 000 plants.

The Wetaskiwin area is rich in grain, coal, oil and cattle. Stan Reynolds' Pioneer Museum displays antique cars, tractors, steam engines, fire engines and airplanes. The Forestburg Collieries and the Battle River Generating Station both give tours of their facilities.

Edmonton, located in the centre of the province, covers 700 square kilometres (270 square miles). It is the capital of Alberta. The Legislative Building, constructed between 1907 and 1912, sits in beautifully landscaped grounds above the North Saskatchewan River. Edmonton has created a system of parks along the river valley that enhances the look of the city and provides recreational areas. Three huge glass pyramids sit on the river flats near the Low Level Bridge. This is the Muttart Conservatory housing tropical, desert and temperate-climate plants plus special displays. The small Valley Zoo, with about 360 animals, is upstream on the opposite side of the river. Edmonton's historical roots are depicted at Fort Edmonton and the Provincial Museum.

Above: Edmonton, with its constantly changing skyline, is Canada's most northerly major city. *Middle:* The Muttart Conservatory, in downtown Edmonton, displays plants of arid, tropical and temperate climates. *Right and far right:* The West Edmonton Mall is a city-within-a-city covering over 45 ha (110 acres), containing the world's largest indoor amusement park, two indoor pools, a skating rink, miniature golf and hundreds of shops.

Edmonton's streets, theatres and concert halls ring with music from the many festivals the city hosts. August's Folk Music Festival and Fringe Theatre Event follow July's Jazz Extravaganza. The largest celebration is Klondike Days when Edmontonians relive the Klondike Gold Rush. Heritage Days are held on the first Saturday and Sunday in August to celebrate Edmonton's ethnic richness.

Local, national and international tourists come to visit West Edmonton Mall, sometimes humorously called the eighth wonder of the world. The mall blends an amusement park with 800 shops, 11 department stores, 110 restaurants, 19 movie theatres and a hotel. The indoor water park brings sun and surf to this northern city even in January.

When Edmontonians want to ski or hike in the mountains, they head west to Jasper. Jasper, a year-round vacation resort, offers skiing, hiking, mountain-climbing, golfing, fishing, white-water

Running 230 km (142 mi.) from Lake Louise to the town of Jasper, the Icefields Parkway offers spectacular views of glaciers, mountain peaks and waterfalls.

Right: Jasper Park Lodge and the aptly named Lac Beauvert. The park and the town of Jasper are named after Jasper Hawes, a North West Company trader who built a post in the area in 1801. *Far right*: Special tour buses take sightseers on a spectacular ride across the Athabasca Glacier.

canoeing, trail-riding, shopping and entertainment. To appreciate the splendour of the Rockies, a tramway trip up The Whistlers Mountain is a must. To get a close look at what is left of the ice age, people can take a Snocoach ride out onto the Columbia Ice Field. After a day of activity, Miette Hot Springs, the warmest springs in the Canadian Rockies, is the place to soak tired muscles.

East of Edmonton, Elk Island National Park, Vegreville and Cold Lake are the sites of very different attractions. Elk Island Park provides boating and hiking opportunities and protects a small herd of buffalo. A huge *pysanka* (Ukrainian Easter egg) is on display in Vegreville. Cold Lake is the site of one of the biggest Canadian Forces bases in Canada with some of the most sophisticated computer equipment in Alberta.

The junction of the Peace and Smoky rivers. The Peace was for many years a main artery of the fur trade. Its fertile valley is now known for bumper grain and canola crops. *Inset*: This giant *pysanka* (Easter egg) honours the Ukrainian pioneers who settled the Vegreville area east of Edmonton.

Peace River in the northern part of the province is situated in a deep valley that is a yellow and orange wonderland when the aspen and saskatoon leaves turn colour in the fall. Peace River is the supply centre for a large farming community. It is also the site of the Daishowa pulp mill which uses aspen trees to make pulp. West of Peace River is Grande Prairie, one of the two cities in northern Alberta. The Grande Prairie area grows bumper grain crops.

High Level, north of Peace River on the Mackenzie Highway, is the site of a computerized mill that uses 200 truckloads of logs per day. Across the Peace River from High Level is one of the oldest European settlements in Alberta — Fort Vermilion. It began as a North West Company fur-trading post in 1788.

Fort McMurray and Wood Buffalo National Park occupy the north east corner of Alberta. The city of Fort McMurray has grown as oil sands along the Athabasca River have been developed. The

Oil Sands Interpretive Centre provides a high-tech look at the history and technology of the oil sands. Wood Buffalo National Park not only shelters the last large herds of wood bison and plains buffalo, it is also the nesting grounds for the endangered whooping crane.

The combination of Alberta's natural beauty, abundant resources, and multicultural population has produced a friendly dynamic

Right: Bison grazing in Wood Buffalo National Park in northeastern Alberta. The huge park was established in 1922 to protect North America's last herd of wood bison.
Below: Fort McMurray, which began life as a fur trading post

province. The spectacular scenery of mountains, foothills, forests and plains delights residents and visitors alike. Many Albertans welcome the development of their natural resources, but many want assurances that the province's forests, wildlife, clean water and air will be available for future generations.

From before the days of the fur trade to present time, Albertans' boldness, tenacity and belief in the strength of the individual have enriched the province and Canada. One of the challenges facing Albertans today, is to balance industrial development with environmental protection. Another is to utilize the strengths of Alberta's many cultures while maintaining tolerance and understanding of differing values and traditions.

Rocky Mountain sunset in Waterton Lakes National Park

Facts
at a Glance

General Information

Provincehood: September 1, 1905

Origin of Name: Named for Queen Victoria's fourth daughter, Princess Louise Caroline Alberta, wife of the Marquis of Lorne, Governor General of Canada 1878-83.

Capital City: Edmonton — began as a fur fort in 1795; incorporated as a town in 1892; became a city in 1904; chosen as the capital city in 1905.

Provincial Nicknames: Alberta is sometimes called the Princess Province, the Energy Province or the Sunshine Province. Princess Province comes from the origin of its name, the abundance of its resources and the wealth it has generated. Energy Province comes from the fact that the province contains over 80 percent of Canada's oil and natural gas reserves. Alberta is called the Sunshine Province because it has more sunny days than any other Canadian province.

Provincial Flag: The flag features the coat of arms on a blue background, and it originated from a banner designed for Canada's Centennial celebrations in 1967. It was adopted in 1968. The provincial coat of arms, adopted in 1907, is shield-shaped with the Cross of St. George at the top, mountains and foothills in the centre and a field of wheat at the bottom. The cross of St. George represents Alberta's historic ties with Great Britain. The mountains and foothills symbolize the Canadian Rockies and the wheat pictures Alberta's major agricultural crop.

Motto: *Fortis et Liber* which means Strong and Free

Provincial Bird: Great Horned Owl, adopted 1977

Provincial Flower: Wild Rose

Provincial Tree: Lodgepole Pine

Population

Population: 2 545 553 (1991 census)

Population Density: 3.8 persons per km^2 (9.8 per sq. mi.)

Population Growth: Alberta's population has had spurts of growth followed by periods of little change.

Population Growth

Year	Population
1901	73 000
1921	588 000
1941	796 200
1961	1 331 900
1971	1 627 874
1981	2 237 300
1991	2 545 553

(Source: Alberta Bureau of Statistics)

Geography

Alberta lies in western Canada between the 110th and 120th meridians of longitude and the 49th and 60th parallels of latitude. Alberta shares borders with British Columbia, the Northwest Territories, Saskatchewan and the State of Montana.

Highest Point: Mount Columbia, 3747 m (12 293 ft.) high, is on the Alberta-British Columbia border between Jasper and Banff national parks.

Lowest Point: In north-eastern Alberta, around Lake Athabasca and along the Slave River, the land is only 208 m (686 ft.) above sea level.

Area: Alberta covers 661 185 km² (255 285 sq. mi.) of which 97 percent is land, and 3 percent water.

Rank in size: Alberta is the fourth-largest Canadian province and the largest Prairie Province.

Rivers: The extreme southern part of Alberta is drained by the Milk River which flows through Montana into the Missouri River, joins the Mississippi River and ends in the Gulf of Mexico. The land from Edmonton to south of Lethbridge and Medicine Hat is drained by the North and South Saskatchewan rivers. The North Saskatchewan rises in the Rocky Mountain's Columbia Ice Fields between Jasper and Banff national parks. The North and South Saskatchewan rivers combine and enter Lake Winnipeg in Manitoba, which is connected to Hudson Bay by the Nelson River.

From Edmonton north, the province is drained by the Hay, Peace and Athabasca rivers into Great Slave Lake and then into the Mackenzie River system which leads to the Arctic Ocean.

Lakes: Alberta's largest lakes are Lake Claire, Lesser Slave Lake, the one-third of Lake Athabasca that lies in Alberta and Lake Bistcho. There are numerous small lakes in the mountains and on the plains, many of which are used for fishing and water sports.

Topography: Alberta has four topographical regions: mountains, foothills, plains and the Canadian Shield. A tip of the Canadian Shield lies in the northeast corner of Alberta. Most of the region is less than 300 m (1000 ft.) above sea level.

Plains: The plains, which cover about two-thirds of the province, contain many ranges of hills that vary in height from 214 to 762 m (700 ft. to 2500 ft.). The northern plains are forested except around Grande Prairie and the Fairview-Grimshaw area. The central plains contain the richest soils and support much of the farming industry. The southern plains are treeless, and drier than the central and northern plains.

Foothills: The foothills are long ridges and hills that run parallel to the eastern face of the Rocky Mountains. They are from 1000 to 1900 m (3300 to 6200 ft.) The higher hills are covered with lodgepole pine and white spruce. Aspen, poplar and birch grow below 1200 m (3900 ft.). In the northern foothills, black spruce and tamarack grow in the valleys and on the lower slopes. The undergrowth consists of shrubs and bushes (willows, alders and blueberry) and flowers (wild rose and fireweed). Winter chinooks often melt much of the snow so that the foothills, especially in the south, are good for cattle ranching.

Mountains: The Alberta section of the Rocky Mountains is part of the many mountain chains or Cordillera that extend from Alaska to the southern tip of South America. The highest mountain peak in Alberta is Mount Columbia at 3747 m (12 293 ft.).

The Twins in Jasper National Park rise to 3683 m (12 085 ft.) and 3558 m (11 675 ft.). About another thirty mountains are over 3000 m (10 000 ft.).

Trees do not grow above 2300 m (7500 ft.). Only mosses, lichens and alpine shrubs grow above the tree line, where ptarmigan and mountain goats live. Goats stay on the higher elevations except in very bad weather, while bighorn sheep move onto the lower slopes in autumn. Mountain caribou live in the zone just below the tree line.

Climate: Alberta has long cold winters and short, warm summers. The weather is influenced by latitude, altitude, the Rocky Mountains

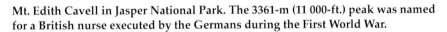

Mt. Edith Cavell in Jasper National Park. The 3361-m (11 000-ft.) peak was named for a British nurse executed by the Germans during the First World War.

and the wind direction. Warm air from the Pacific Ocean keeps Alberta warmer than the other Prairie Provinces.

Winter dangers include intense cold, windchill and blizzards. The coldest winter temperatures are found from Edmonton north. The average January temperatures are, for Edmonton -13° C (8° F) and -10° C (14° F) in Medicine Hat. The lowest temperature ever recorded in Alberta was -61° C (-78° F) at Fort Vermilion on January 11, 1911.

The direction of the wind determines the temperature and the amount of precipitation received. Major winter storms usually come on a north wind. Chinook winds from the west can raise temperatures in some parts of Alberta dramatically. Since snow develops where warm moist Pacific air and cold Arctic air meet, the mountains and foothills get the most snowfall.

Alberta gets most of its precipitation in the summer. June and July have an average of 14 days of rain. April and October usually have the lowest number of days of rain or snow. The north central part of the province plus a strip along the mountains receives 38 to 51 cm (15 to 20 in.) of precipitation per year. The area north of Peace River and south and east of Edmonton receives only about two-thirds that amount. Thunder showers often occur in the afternoons. Sometimes the thunder clouds contain hail and occasionally they generate a tornado.

The warmest temperatures in summer are in the southeast; the coolest are in the north and along the mountains. The average summer temperature is 15° C (60° F) in Grande Prairie and 21° C (70° F) in Medicine Hat. Almost all of Alberta has more than 2000 hours of sunshine a year.

Nature

Trees: Aspen, pine, white and black spruce, tamarack, fir, balsam spruce, poplar and birch all grow in Alberta. The undergrowth consists of willows, alder, saskatoon, chokecherry, pin cherry, honeysuckle, wild rose, juniper and bearberry.

Wild Plants: Alberta is blessed with a wealth of wild plants including many species of fern, grass, herb and orchid, plus wildflowers such as anemone, marigold, larkspur, fireweed, violet, buttercup and bluebell.

Animals: Alberta has a diversity of wildlife inhabiting the different vegetation zones. Animals inhabiting the southeastern grasslands include ground squirrels, cottontails, kangaroo rats, pronghorns, white-tailed deer, mule deer, grasshopper mice, beavers and voles. The grassland predators are coyote and red fox.

In the parkland and boreal forest, there are snowshoe hare, coyote, lynx, red fox, muskrat, beaver, mink, weasel, wapiti, moose, white-tailed deer, black bear, skunk, porcupine, badger, fisher and wolf. Moose, wolf,

Cougars, once common in much of the country, now survive mainly in forested mountain regions.

grizzly bear, black bear, lynx and snowshoe hare particularly like the Swan Hills.

Moose, white-tailed deer, elk, mountain sheep, mountain goats, woodland and mountain caribou, grizzly bear, black bear, mule deer, cougar, coyote and ground squirrels live in the foothills and on the mountain slopes. On the higher mountain slopes, there are mountain caribou, wolverine, wolf, grizzly bear, mountain goat, mountain sheep, moose, mule deer, hoary marmot, marten, pika, ground squirrels, chipmunk and deermouse.

Birds: Alberta's numerous ponds, sloughs and lakes provide habitat for a variety of water birds. There are loons, grebes, pelicans, herons, swans, geese and ducks. Hawks, bald and golden eagles, ospreys, turkey vultures and falcons hunt their prey on the prairie, in the foothills

and mountains. Varieties of grouse, partridge, ptarmigan, coots, yellowlegs, dowitchers, plovers, sandpipers, avocets, willets, godwit, gulls and terns are found, as well as sandhill cranes.

There are smaller birds such as pigeons, mourning doves, cuckoos, owls, nighthawks, swifts, hummingbirds, kingfishers, flickers, woodpeckers, sapsuckers, flycatchers, larks, swallows and purple martins. Then there are members of the crow family such as crows, ravens, magpies and jays. Nutcrackers, nuthatches, dippers, rock wrens, thrushes, kinglets, waxwings, shrikes, starlings, vireos, warblers, sparrows, blackbirds, orioles, meadowlarks, grackles, cowbirds, tanagers, grosbeaks, finches, juncoes and snow buntings are found in the province.

Fish: Sturgeon, arctic grayling, whitefish, lake trout, rainbow trout, Dolly Varden, pike, minnows, suckers, perch, sculpin, catfish, codfish and stickleback swim in Alberta lakes and rivers.

Government

Organization: Alberta's laws are made by 83 elected Members of the Legislative Assembly. Usually the political party that elects the most members forms the government and the leader of that party becomes the premier. Elected members from other political parties form the Opposition. The premier and the cabinet run the government. Cabinet members are chosen from the party in power by the premier. Albertans may vote in a provincial election if they are Canadian citizens, 18 years of age or older and have been resident in Alberta for 6 months before election date.

Courts: There are two courts in Alberta: the Court of Queen's Bench and the Provincial Court. The Court of Queen's Bench has two branches, the Trials Division and the Appeals Division. It is the highest court in Alberta. Judges for the Court of Queen's Bench are appointed by the federal government. The provincial court judges are appointed by the province.

Local Government: Alberta is divided into urban and rural municipalities. Urban municipalities include cities, towns, villages and summer villages or resort areas. They are administered by an elected mayor and council. Rural municipalities include municipal districts, counties, and improvement districts. Rural municipalities are administered by elected councilors, except for improvement districts which are governed directly by Alberta Municipal Affairs. County school boards are committees of the County Council, while in municipal districts, they are separate elected bodies.

Municipalities provide police and fire protection, garbage disposal, sewage treatment, water, gas and electric utilities, road maintenance, public transportation, parks and recreational services. Funds are derived from local property taxes and provincial government grants.

Education

The provincial government and local school boards share the responsibility for providing basic public education in Alberta. Alberta Education is responsible for teacher qualification, and curriculum. Local school boards operate schools and employ teachers. Funds are obtained from local property taxes and provincial government grants. There are about half a million students in Alberta's schools.

Post-secondary education is supported by government grants, tuition fees and private grants. Alberta has five universities; Calgary, Edmonton, Lethbridge, Athabasca (distance-learning) and the Banff Centre School of Fine Arts.

Albertans have a choice of 11 public and 4 private colleges, plus 3 technical institutes and 6 hospital based schools of nursing. Four vocational centres and approximately 50 volunteer literacy programs help learners upgrade their basic skills. There are 85 further education councils which arrange special interest courses.

Economy and Industry

Alberta's economy depends on the production and sale of cattle, wheat, canola, barley and other agricultural products; petroleum products, services and manufactured goods. Service Industries made up 63 percent of all the goods and services sold in the province in 1990. The remainder of the goods and services sold come from energy, 16 percent; manufacturing 9 percent; construction 6 percent; agriculture 5 percent; and forestry 1 percent.

Communications: Daily newspapers are *The Calgary Herald, The Calgary Sun, The Edmonton Journal, The Edmonton Sun, Fort McMurray Today, The Grand Prairie Daily Herald Tribune, The Lethbridge Herald, The Medicine Hat News,* and *The Red Deer Advocate. The Globe and Mail* is sent via satellite and printed in Calgary, where *The Financial Post* also has a bureau. In 1990 there were 150 weekly newspapers published by smaller centres, interest groups and businesses.

The province has 118 television stations and 174 radio stations. The CBC network has radio stations in Edmonton and Calgary, but only Edmonton has a CBC television station. CKUA, which is provincially owned, is utilized by ACCESS for educational broadcasts.

Transportation: Railways were the first public transport to make an impact on Alberta. Today, the CPR

The High Level Bridge at Lethbridge is the longest, highest rail trestle in the world. *Inset*: **Petroglyphs carved by the Natives hundreds of years ago on the sandstone cliffs of Writing-on-Stone Provincial Park, southeast of Lethbridge**

Highway through farm country in the foothills of southern Alberta. *Inset*: **A nineteenth-century stagecoach is one of the many relics of bygone days to be seen at Fort Edmonton Park.**

serves southern Alberta, the CNR central Alberta and the Alberta Resources Railway, the Northern Alberta Railway and the Great Slave Railway transport goods in the north. Railways are vital to the transport of Alberta grain to port facilities on the east and west coasts. Pipelines carry oil and gas to eastern Canada, the Pacific coast and the United States.

Highways became more important after the Second World War as industry developed. Today, Alberta has 153 873 k (95 600 mi.) of highways and roads, 21 550 k (13 390 mi.) paved and 109 763 k (68 200 mi.) gravelled. Alberta's most heavily travelled road is Highway 2 between Edmonton and Calgary. Another busy highway, the Trans-Canada, runs through Medicine Hat, Calgary and Banff. The Yellowhead Highway connects Saskatchewan and British Columbia through Lloydminster, Edmonton and Jasper. The Mackenzie carries traffic from Peace River to the Northwest Territories. Highway 4 south from Lethbridge joins Interstate 15 in Montana.

Air traffic is handled by Alberta's two international airports located at Edmonton and Calgary. Regular service to other provinces, the United States, Europe, Asia and Australia is provided by Air Canada, Canadian Airlines International, American, America West, Delta, KLM, Northwest and United airlines. Canadian Airlines and Time Air provide service within Alberta.

Arts and Recreation

Museums: Alberta's museums include natural history, human history and science exhibits. The Royal Tyrrell Museum in Drumheller exhibits dinosaurs and other fossils. The Provincial Museum in Edmonton is a combination of a natural history and a historical museum. The Glenbow Museum in Calgary, the Galt Museum in Lethbridge, and many small town museums such as the one in Girouxville display artifacts from Native and pioneer Alberta. The Museum of the Regiments has collected items from Canada's armed forces participation in war and peace-keeping activities. Many historical parks, restored sites and replicas tell the history of the province. Some of these are Heritage Park, Fort Calgary, Fort Edmonton, Fort Macleod, Fort Whoop-up, Dunvegan and the Ukrainian Cultural Heritage Village.

Libraries: Public libraries are funded by the provincial government. Edmonton and Calgary have

Hoodoos near Drumheller

main libraries with several community branches. For example, Calgary has a Central Library and fifteen branch libraries, for which circulation in 1989 was over 8.3 million items. Universities, colleges, technical, public and separate schools have their own provincially funded libraries. There are some private library collections such as oil company libraries, Glenbow Historical Library and Archives and the Arctic Institute of North America Library at the University of Calgary.

Performing Arts: The provincial government supports performing artists through grants from the Alberta Foundation for the Performing Arts. Most professional performing artists work in Edmonton and Calgary. Performing companies in Calgary include the Calgary Philharmonic, Calgary Opera Company, Chamber Music Society of Calgary, Calgary Festival Chorus, and the Early Music Society of Calgary. Productions by the Loose Moose Theatre, Lunchbox Theatre, Theatre Calgary, Stage West, Glenmore Dinner Theatre, Pleiades Theatre, Pumphouse Theatre, and the University Theatre are enjoyed by Calgarians. In the capital city, the Edmonton Symphony Orchestra, Alberta Ballet Company, Alberta Contemporary Dance Theatre, Citadel Theatre, Northern Light Theatre, Theatre Network, Theatre 3, and Stage West entertain Edmontonians.

Sports and Recreation: Edmonton and Calgary have rival professional CFL football and NHL hockey teams. Both the Edmonton Oilers and the Calgary Flames hockey teams have been Stanley Cup winners. Eager to represent Alberta in the Grey Cup games are the Edmonton Eskimo and Calgary Stampeder football teams. The two cities also support the Calgary Cannons and Edmonton Trappers baseball clubs.

Albertans have excelled at international competitions. Four-time World Champion figure skater Kurt Browning, medal-winning skiers Karen Percy, Karrin Lee-Gartner and Ken Read, Olympic swimmers Becky and Graham Smith, Michelle Cameron and Carolyn Waldo, six-time World Champion trap-shooter, Susan Nattrass, and twice Canadian Biathlon Champion Madelaine Bouz are just a few of Alberta's exceptional athletes.

Edmonton, Calgary and several other centres have excellent sports facilities for hockey, football, skiing, biathlon, speed, figure and pleasure skating, luge, bobsledding, curling, track and field and swimming. Some of the more notable facilities are Canada Olympic Park, Olympic Oval and Olympic Saddledome in Calgary; the Northlands Coliseum and Commonwealth Stadium in Edmonton and the many ski slopes and trails in Banff, Jasper, Kananaskis and the Canmore Nordic Centre.

Many Alberta towns and cities hold rodeos and horse races. Edmonton hosts the Canadian Finals Rodeo, Northlands Superodeo, thoroughbred and harness racing. Calgary has the Calgary Stampede as well as thoroughbred and harness racing. Hobbema, Vermilion and many other towns have rodeos. Spruce Meadows, near Calgary, presents three annual show-jumping tournaments that include music, flowers and international competition, in a friendly western setting.

Historic Sights and Landmarks: Some of the historic sights to see in Alberta are: the Mormon Church in Cardston; Head-Smashed-In Buffalo

Left: **Fryatt Creek and Mt. Fryatt, Jasper National Park. The tall, vertical peaks of the Rockies indicate that they are a young mountain range — North America's youngest, in fact.** *Right*: **About 55 km (34 mi.) south of Jasper, the Sunwapta River plunges into a deep canyon, creating a spectacular waterfall.**

Jump; Twelve-Foot Davis's grave in Peace River; the Banff Springs Hotel; Heritage Park in Calgary; the Legislative Building in Edmonton; Fort Edmonton, Fort Macleod and Fort Calgary; John Ware's cabin northeast of Brooks near Dinosaur Provincial Park, Fort Whoop-up; Stephan Stephansson's home southwest of Red Deer; McDougall Church and for horticulturalists, the George Bugnet farm in Rich Valley.

Landmarks include hoodoos sculpted by the wind and water in the Badlands along the Red Deer River; the Columbia Ice Fields, the remnants of Ice Age glaciers, located between Banff and Jasper; the Frank Slide, where part of Turtle Mountain slid down on top of the town of Frank in the Crowsnest Pass; the oil sands at Fort McMurray and, of course, the Rocky Mountains.

Other interesting places to visit are West Edmonton Mall, Calaway Park and Spruce Meadows near Calgary, Jasper, Banff and Waterton national parks, provincial parks, Lake Louise, Sylvan Lake, Lesser Slave Lake, the Japanese Gardens in Lethbridge, the Royal Tyrrell Museum in Drumheller and the giant *pysanka* in Vegreville.

Annual events too good to miss are the Calgary Stampede; Banff Indians Days; Edmonton's Klondike Days; Jazz City; Fringe Theatre Event and Folk Festival; Lethbridge's Whoop-up Days; the Red Deer Air Show and the Hooves of History Cattle Drive to Cochrane.

Important Dates

1754   Anthony Henday visits Alberta region to ask Blackfoot to trade with Hudson's Bay Company

1795   North West Company builds Fort Augustus and the Hudson's Bay Company builds Edmonton House

1840   Reverend Robert Rundle, the first missionary, arrives in the area that is now Alberta

1852   Father Lacombe arrives

1863   Methodist missionaries, George and John McDougall establish a mission at Victoria, now called Pakan, Alberta

1870   The Dominion of Canada buys Rupert's Land from the Hudson's Bay Company

1874   The NWMP builds Fort Macleod and Fort Calgary

1876   Treaty Number 6 signed with the Cree in Central Alberta

1877   Treaty Number 7 signed with Blackfoot, Blood, Peigan, Sarcee and Stoney

1883   CPR tracks reach Calgary

1887   Banff is established as Canada's first national park

1898   The Klondike gold rush brings people to Edmonton, on their way to the Yukon

1899   Treaty Number 8 signed with most Northern Indian bands

1905   Alberta becomes a province. Edmonton is named the capital city; A Liberal, Alexander Rutherford, becomes Alberta's first premier

1914   Oil is discovered at Turner Valley

1916   Women gain the right to vote in Alberta elections

1917   The first women (Louise McKinney and Roberta MacAdams) are elected to the Alberta legislature

1921   The first woman appointed as a Cabinet Minister in the Alberta government is Irene Parlby, Minister Without Portfolio

1929   Five Alberta women ask the Supreme Court of Canada to rule on whether women are "persons" and eligible therefore to be appointed to the Senate. The Court says no, but the Privy Council Judicial Committee says yes.

1935   Alberta elects Canada's first Social Credit government. William Aberhart becomes premier

1947   A major oil field is discovered at Leduc outside Edmonton; economic expansion begins

1958   Pipelines are completed to Ontario and the British Columbia coast

1965	The railway is completed from Grimshaw to Hay River and Pine Point, in the Northwest Territories
1967	The Great Canadian Oil Sands plant begins extracting oil from bituminous sands near Fort McMurray
1967	Native people can vote in Alberta for the first time
1969	The Alberta Resources Railway is completed from Grande Prairie to the Hinton area
1971	A Progressive Conservative government is elected, with Peter Lougheed as premier
1975	The Alberta Heritage Savings Trust Fund is established, setting aside 30 percent of petroleum royalties for the future
1978	Edmonton hosts the eleventh Commonwealth Games
1985	The first woman, Helen Hunley, is appointed Lieutenant-Governor
1986	Premier Lougheed resigns; Don Getty becomes premier
1988	Calgary hosts the Winter Olympic Games
1990	Stan Waters is appointed to the Senate, becoming the first senator in Canadian history to be elected *and* appointed; Walter P. Twinn, Chief of the Sawridge Indian Band and member of the Progressive Conservative Party, is appointed to the Senate
1992	Justice Catherine Anne Fraser is appointed Chief Justice of Alberta. She is the first woman in Canada to hold the top job in a provincial justice system
1993	Conservatives under Ralph Klein win election; new Environmental Protection and Enhancement Act becomes effective

Moraine Lake in Banff National Park is surrounded by the sharp Wenkchemna (a Native word meaning ten) Peaks.

R.B. Bennett

Michelle Cameron

Joe Clark

Crowfoot

Important People

Of the millions of important people who grew from this land or came from other lands to build Alberta, a tiny sample follows:

William Aberhart (1878-1943), born in Ontario, moved to Alberta in 1910; preacher, politician; founded the Social Credit Party and led it to victory in the 1935 provincial election; premier of Alberta 1935-1943

R.B. Bennett (1870-1947), born in Hopewell Hill, New Brunswick; millionaire Calgary lawyer; prime minister of Canada 1930 to 1935. In the Depression, western farmers, who could not afford to buy gas, named their horse drawn cars "Bennett buggies"

Kurt Browning (1966-   ), born in Caroline, Alberta; Men's World Figure Skating Champion four times, 1989, 1990, 1991 and 1993

Pat Burns (1856-1937), born in Oshawa, Ontario; cattle king, philanthropist; began Burns meat-packing business in Calgary in 1890; expanded into eastern Canada, British Columbia, United States, Great Britain and Japan; one of the Big Four who financed the first Calgary Stampede; was named to the Senate in 1931

Michelle Cameron (1962-   ), born in Calgary; won gold medal (with Carolyn Waldo) for synchronized swimming duet in 1988 Olympics

Douglas Cardinal (1934-   ), born in Calgary; the great-grandson of a Blood Indian woman and a European settler; architect; designed the Canadian Museum of Civilization (1989) in Hull, Quebec

Tantoo Cardinal (1951-   ), born in Anzac, near Fort McMurray; actress; became interested in drama while attending high school in Edmonton; starred in *Dances with Wolves*

Joe Clark (1939–   ), born in High River; Member of Parliament for Rocky Mountain and Yellowhead ridings; youngest Prime Minister of Canada from June 4, 1979 to March 2, 1980; External Affairs Minister 1984–91, then Constitutional Affairs Minister until he retired from politics in 1993

James Cornwall (1869-1955), born in Brantford, Ontario; prospector, trader, promoter of the Peace River country; Liberal MLA for Peace River from 1908 to 1912; known as "Peace River Jim"

Crowfoot (1821-1890), born south of the Red Deer River; Chief of the Blackfoot; worked for peace both among tribes and between Natives and newcomers; signed Treaty Number 7, September 22, 1877, for the Blackfoot and devoted the rest of his life to helping his people adjust to a new way of life

Henrietta Muir Edwards (1849-1931), born in Montreal; helped found the National Council of Women and the Victorian Order of Nurses; came to Alberta in 1903; member of Women's Christian Temperance Union; got other WCTU members interested in votes for women; one of "Famous Five" who won the court battle to have women legally designated as "persons"

James Gladstone (1887-1971), born at Mountain Hill; adopted by the Blackfoot; became first Native in the Canadian Senate in 1958; helped get treaty Indians the right to vote in federal elections in 1962; Gladstone Mountain is named for him

Matthew Halton (1904-1956), born at Pincher Creek; reporter for *The Toronto Star*; war correspondent for CBC; author of *Ten Years to Alamein*; as CBC's post-war European correspondent, interviewed world leaders of the forties and fifties

Jan Hudson (1954-1990), born in Calgary; lawyer and author of historical fiction based on Native themes, for children and young adults; has won many awards and been published in many languages

Mel Hurtig (1932-   ), born in Edmonton; opened province's first books-only bookshop in 1955; began Hurtig Publishers in 1972, publishing Canadian books only; fierce fighter for Canada in the political arena; leader of the National Party of Canada, which he founded in 1992

Dr. Mary Percy Jackson (1905-   ), born in England, arrived in Alberta in 1929; employed by Alberta government as the only doctor in a huge territory 120 k (75 mi.) north of Peace River; moved to Keg River with her husband rancher Frank Jackson in 1930; her pay was in berries, moccasins and wild meat until medicare was instituted in the 1960s; retired in 1974; received the Centennial Medal of Canada and Alberta Achievement Award

Alex Janvier (1937-   ), born on the Cold Lake Reserve; graduated Alberta College of Art, Calgary; painter; expresses his concerns and experiences symbolically in brightly coloured lines and shapes

Martha Kostuch (1949-   ), born at Moose Lake, Minnesota; veterinarian, active environmentalist, friend of the Oldman River, concerned with the environment, human and animal health

William Kurelek (1927-1977), born in Whitford, Alberta; artist and author; realistic paintings

Henrietta Muir Edwards

James Gladstone

Mel Hurtig

Alex Janvier

William Kurelek

Peter Lougheed

Grant MacEwan

Nellie McClung

show Ukrainian homesteading heritage

Norman Kwong (1929-   ), born in Calgary; businessman, one of the owners of Calgary Flames hockey team, football player (known as "the China Clipper"); played for Edmonton Eskimos and Calgary Stampeders; CFL all-star five times, Schenley Award winner 1955 and 1956, Athlete of the Year 1956; Alberta Sports Hall of Fame 1987

k.d. lang (1961-   ), born in Consort; singer; several-time winner of Juno and Grammy awards; controversial commercial advocating vegetarianism made her unpopular with Alberta ranchers and radio stations

Sheridan and Julia Lawrence (1870-1952 and 1879-1974), farmers, ranchers, traders, freighters at Fort Vermilion; arrived as missionaries' children in 1886; married August 21, 1900; raised seven sons and eight daughters; fed, housed and nursed many northern travellers; a cairn honouring their achievements has been erected in Peace River

Peter Lougheed (1928-   ), third-generation Albertan born in Calgary; lawyer; became leader of the Progressive Conservatives in March 1965; elected premier in 1971; established Heritage Trust Fund

Roberta MacAdams (1881-1959), born in Sarnia, Ontario; nursed in the armed forces; soldiers' vote elected her to Legislature in 1917, one of the first two women elected in Canada; first woman in British empire to introduce a bill

Grant MacEwan (1902-   ), born near Brandon, Manitoba; writer and newspaper columnist; came to Alberta in the 1950s; was Mayor of Calgary, leader of the Provincial Liberal party, Lieutenant-Governor of Alberta

Colonel James Farquharson Macleod (1836-1894), born Isle of Skye, Scotland, came to Canada 1842; came west on the NWMP Great March; a friend of Chief Crowfoot; helped NWMP earn respect and trust of the Indians; became a magistrate in Pincher Creek when he retired from the police force

Nellie McClung (1873-1951), born in Chatsworth, Ontario, moved to Alberta 1914; author, suffragist, politician; one of "Famous Five" who got women legally recognized as "Persons"; member of the Alberta Legislature from 1921 to 1926; first woman on CBC board of governors; Canadian delegate to League of Nations

Grant McConachie (1909-1965), born at Hamilton, Ontario, moved to Alberta, 1910; pioneered mail, freight and passenger flights into the north; began an airline company that became part of CP Air; became President of CP Air in 1947; initiated flights to Australia, Asia and South America; first to fly transpolar route to Europe

Louise McKinney (1868-1931), born in Frankville, Ontario, came to Alberta in 1903; schoolteacher, suffragist, president of Women's Christian Temperance Union; one of the first two women elected to a legislature in 1917; one of "Famous Five"

Euphemia (Betty) McNaught (1901-   ), born in Ontario; artist; came to Beaverlodge homestead by oxcart over the Edson trail in 1912; painter, sculptor and teacher; paints watercolour and ink landscapes and pioneer scenes

Ernest C. Manning (1908-   ), born at Carnduff, Saskatchewan; Social Credit Premier of Alberta from 1943 to 1968, first Social Credit member to be appointed to Canadian Senate in 1970

Preston Manning (1942-   ), born in Edmonton; politician; founded the Reform Party of Canada in 1987; calling for a balanced budget, Senate reform and a process that would make politicians more accountable to the public, led his party to an electoral breakthrough in the 1993 federal election

Roland Michener (1900-1991), born in Lacombe, Alberta; grew up in Red Deer; lawyer, politician, Member of Parliament; Speaker of the House of Commons, and High Commissioner to India; Governor General of Canada from 1967 to 1974

Emily Murphy (1868-1933), born in Cookstown, Ontario, came to Alberta in 1907; author, suffragist, magistrate; campaigned for passage of Dower Act; one of the "Famous Five;" first woman police magistrate in British Empire

Susan Nattrass (1950-   ), born in Medicine Hat; Woman's World Champion trap-shooter six times; in 1976 Olympics, competed using same standards as men, first woman to do so; Athlete of the Year 1981; Order of Canada

Charles Sherwood Noble (1873-1957), agricultural conservationist, farmer, homesteader at Claresholm; grew world record crops of flax, oats and wheat; invented the Noble Drill and Noble Blade to replace traditional ploughs and conserve water

J. Percy Page (1887-1973), teacher, high-school principal, coach of the Commercial Grads girls' basketball team which had the best record in Canadian sports history; House leader of the Progressive Conservatives, appointed Lieutenant-Governor of Alberta 1959-1966

Louise Mckinney

Roland Michener

Susan Nattrass

Charles Sherwood Noble

Irene Parlby

A.C. Rutherford

Ralph Garvin Steinhauer

Carolyn Waldo

Irene Parlby (1868-1965), born in London, England; suffragist, politician; one of the organizers and first president of the United Farm Women of Alberta; MLA and cabinet minister 1921-1935; one of the "Famous Five"

A.C. Rutherford (1857-1941), born at Osgood, Canada West; appointed Alberta's first premier, elected two months later; chose Edmonton as capital city; established the University of Alberta; chose site for Legislative Building; established Alberta Government Telephones; helped found the Historical Society of Alberta; Chancellor of the University of Alberta, 1927-1941

Ralph Garvin Steinhauer (1905-   ), born at Morley, Alberta; farmer, Indian leader; founded Indian Association of Alberta; president of Indian Development Corporation; Lieutenant-Governor of Alberta 1974-1979, the first Native to so serve

Stephan Stephansson (1853-1927), born in Iceland; poet, farmer in the Markerville area for forty years; Iceland named him poet laureate in 1917

Walter P. Twinn(1934-   ), Chief of the Sawridge Indian Band since 1966; received an honorary doctorate degree from Athabasca University in 1986 for his contributions to Alberta; appointed to the Canadian Senate, 1990

Carolyn Waldo (1964-   ), born in Montreal, lives in Calgary; synchronized swimmer, won a silver medal in 1984 Olympics and two gold in 1988 Olympics

John Ware (1845-1905), born a slave in South Carolina, came to Alberta 1882, on a cattle drive. Rancher, champion steer wrestler and a horse trainer

Stanley Waters (1920-1991), born in Winnipeg, Manitoba; attended University of Alberta; following distinguished military and business careers, became Canada's first "elected" Senator on June 19, 1990

Guy Weadick (1885-1953), born in Rochester, New York; originator of the Calgary Stampede; planned and organized the first parade and rodeo in 1912, the second in 1919; amalgamated the Stampede with the Calgary Exhibition in 1923; arena director until 1932

Henry Wise Wood (1860-1941), born in Missouri, came to Alberta in 1905; helped thirty thousand farmers organize the United Farmers of Alberta and found the Alberta Wheat Pool in 1923

Premiers of Alberta

Name	Party	Years
Alexander Cameron Rutherford	Liberal	1905-1910
Arthur Lewis Sifton	Liberal	1910-1917
Charles Stewart	Liberal	1917-1921
Herbert Greenfield	United Farmers of Alberta	1921-1925
John Edward Brownlee	United Farmers of Alberta	1925-1934
Richard Gavin Reid	United Farmers of Alberta	1934-1935
William Aberhart	Social Credit	1935-1943
Ernest Charles Manning	Social Credit	1943-1968
Harry Edwin Strom	Social Credit	1968-1971
Peter Lougheed	Conservative	1971-1986
Donald Ross Getty	Conservative	1986-1992
Ralph Klein	Conservative	1992-

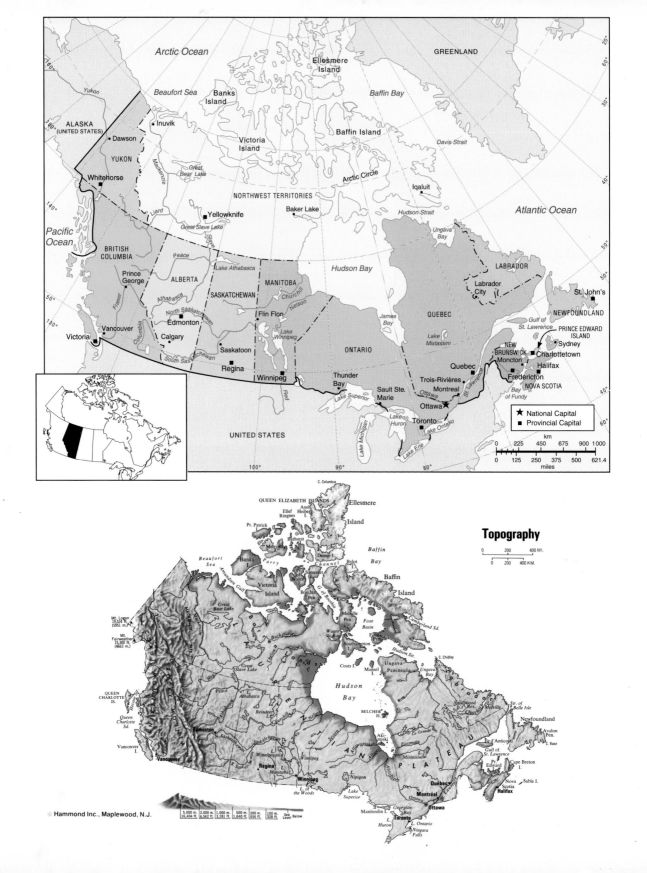

Arctic Ocean

GREENLAND

Ellesmere
Island

Beaufort Sea   Banks
Island   Baffin Bay

ALASKA   Inuvik
(UNITED STATES)

Dawson   Baffin Island

YUKON   Victoria
                Island   Davis Strait

Whitehorse   Great
                Bear Lake   Arctic Circle

                                                Iqaluit   Atlantic Ocean

Yellowknife   Baker Lake   Hudson Strait

Pacific   NORTHWEST TERRITORIES
Ocean
                Great Slave Lake   Ungava
                                                Bay   LABRADOR

BRITISH   Hudson Bay   St. John's
COLUMBIA   Peace   Labrador
                                                                City   NEWFOUNDLAND
Prince   Lake Athabasca MANITOBA
George   ALBERTA   SASKATCHEWAN   QUEBEC   Gulf of
                                                                                St. Lawrence PRINCE EDWARD
                Athabasca   James   ISLAND
                                                Bay   Lake   Sydney
Vancouver   Edmonton   Flin Flon   Mistassini   NEW   Charlottetown
                                                                                BRUNSWICK
Victoria   Calgary   Lake   ONTARIO   Moncton   Halifax
                                Winnipeg   Quebec   Fredericton
                Saskatoon   Trois-Rivières NOVA SCOTIA
                                                               Montreal   Bay
                Regina   Winnipeg   of Fundy
                                                Thunder   Ottawa
                                                Bay   Sault Ste.
                                                               Marie   ★ National Capital
                                Red   Lake Superior   ■ Provincial Capital
UNITED STATES   Lake   Toronto
                                               Huron   Lake Ontario   km
                                Lake Michigan   0   225 450 675 900 1000
                                               Lake Erie

                                                                              0 125 250 375 500 621.4
                                                                                     miles

Topography

QUEEN ELIZABETH ISLANDS   Ellesmere
                           Island
                Axel
Ellef   Heiberg
Ringnes   I.

Pr. Patrick   Baffin
                Melville   Bay
Pr. Patrick   I.
                                      Baffin

Beaufort   Banks   Island
Sea   I.

                Victoria
                Island

Mt. Logan   Great
19,524 ft.   Bear Lake
(5951 m.)
                                      Foxe
Mt.   Great   Basin
Fairweather   Slave Lake
15,300 ft.
(4663 m.)   Southampton
                                      I.

QUEEN   Hudson   Ungava
CHARLOTTE   Bay   Bay
IS.
                Peace

Queen   Newfoundland
Charlotte   Avalon
Sd.   Pen.

                Edmonton   BELCHER
                                     IS.

Vancouver   Nova
I.   Scotia
                Saskatchewan   Gulf of   Sable I.
Vancouver   Regina   St. Lawrence
                                     Winnipeg   Pr.
                                                         Edward   Cape Breton
                Winnipeg   L.   I.
                L.   Nipigon
                of the   Lake   Québec
                Woods   Superior
                                                        Montréal
                                                        Ottawa
                                    Manitoulin   Toronto
                                    I.   Georgian   L. Ontario
                                            Bay
                                    Huron   Niagara
                                                        Falls

© Hammond Inc., Maplewood, N.J.

5,000 m. 2,000 m. 1,000 m. 500 m. 200 m. 100 m. Sea
16,404 ft. 6,562 ft. 3,281 ft. 1,640 ft. 656 ft. 328 ft. Level Below

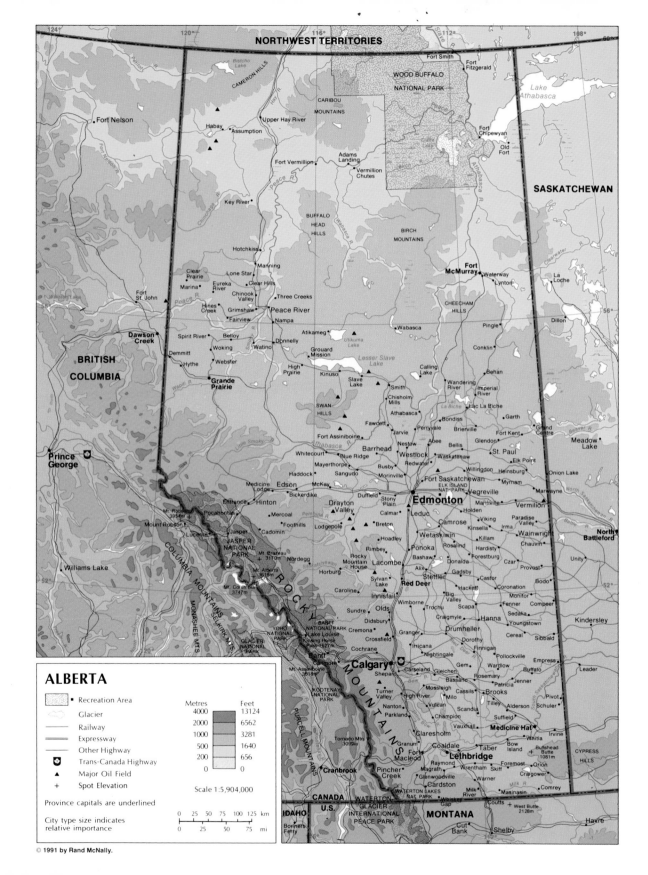

ALBERTA

Legend:

- ▨ ▪ Recreation Area
- ◌ Glacier
- Railway
- Expressway
- Other Highway
- ⬡ Trans-Canada Highway
- ▲ Major Oil Field
- + Spot Elevation

Province capitals are underlined

City type size indicates relative importance

Metres	Feet
4000	13124
2000	6562
1000	3281
500	1640
200	656
0	0

Scale 1:5,904,000

0 25 50 75 100 125 km

0 25 50 75 mi

© 1991 by Rand McNally.

AVERAGE ANNUAL RAINFALL

There are less than 20 inches—500 mm—of rainfall each year in most of Alberta.

Mm		Inches
250-355	1	10-14
355-455	2	14-18
455-560	3	18-22
560-660	4	22-26

Figures within areas are for identification purposes only.

GROWING SEASON

Most of Alberta has less than three frost-free months a year.

Average Number of Days in Frost-Free Period

1	20-40
2	40-60
3	60-80
4	80-100
5	100-120
6	120-140

Figures within areas are for identification purposes only.

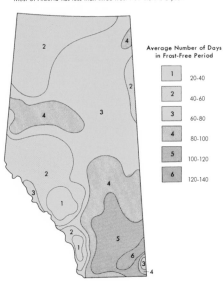

ECONOMY AND AGRICULTURE

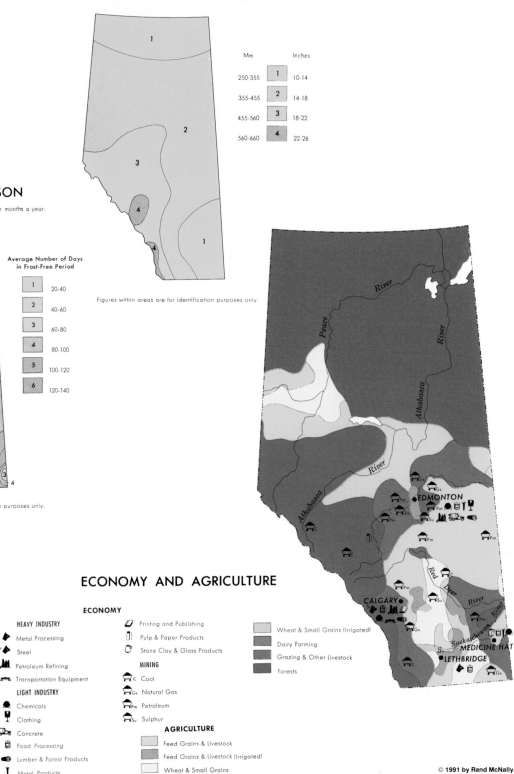

ECONOMY

HEAVY INDUSTRY
- Metal Processing
- St Steel
- Petroleum Refining
- Transportation Equipment

LIGHT INDUSTRY
- Chemicals
- Clothing
- Concrete
- Food Processing
- Lumber & Forest Products
- Metal Products

- Printing and Publishing
- Pulp & Paper Products
- Stone Clay & Glass Products

MINING
- C Coal
- Gs Natural Gas
- Pm Petroleum
- Su Sulphur

AGRICULTURE
- Feed Grains & Livestock
- Feed Grains & Livestock (Irrigated)
- Wheat & Small Grains
- Wheat & Small Grains (Irrigated)
- Dairy Farming
- Grazing & Other Livestock
- Forests

© 1991 by Rand McNally.

Index

About the Author

Edna Bakken was born in Peace River, Alberta. After finishing her studies, she worked as a lab technician in Edmonton, then married and returned to Peace River where her two daughters were born. In 1972, she earned a B.Ed. from the University of Calgary. While working as a teacher-librarian in Calgary public schools, she wrote four books and helped produce resources for various social studies topics. Edna now lives with her husband near Bearberry, in a log house which the family built, and is a volunteer literacy teacher in the Sundre School.

Picture Acknowledgments

Front cover, 2-3, 16 (inset), 98 (left), 121, Fotopic/**The Stock Market Inc., Toronto**; 4, 12 (bottom), 13 (top), 99, 100 (top and bottom), C. Wallis/**FotoLex, Calgary**; 5, 85 (right), C. Harris/**First Light**; 6, 80 (left), 82 (bottom and bottom right), 92 (bottom right), 96 (top), R. Watts, **First Light**; 8-9, 57, 63 (bottom and middle left), 68 (top), 79 (bottom right), 89 (inset), 91 (top left and bottom left), 93 (right), 96 (middle), 101, 109, 111, T. Kitchin/**First Light**; 11 (background), 86-87, The Photo Source/**Superstock**; 11 (inset left), 16 (left), 17 (inset), 18 (insets left and top right), 19 (insets), 20 (top left and right, bottom right), 21 (top left and right), 23 (bottom right), 26 (all), 27, 59 (bottom left and right), 60 (bottom right), 61 (inset), 63 (inset left and bottom right), 64 (both), 71 (inset), 72, 73 (both), 78 (both), 79 (top right), 82 (top left), 90 (both), 91 (middle left and bottom right), 92 (left, top middle and top right), 93 (left), 95 (both), 99 (inset), 109 (inset), 113 (left), back cover, Robin White/**FotoLex, Calgary**; 11 (inset right), M. Farquhar/**Focus**; 12 (top)_, Anne Gransden/**Superstock**; 13 (bottom), 55, Mick Roessler/**Superstock**; 15 (top), 17 (left), 60 (bottom left), 89 (left), 110, Fotopic/**Superstock**; 15 (bottom), U. Wompa/**Superstock**; 15 (inset right), Donald Denton/**First Light**; 17 (top right and bottom), 18 (inset middle and bottom), 102 (bird, flower), 107, **Bill Ivy**; 18-19, Steve Short/**First Light**; 20 (bottom left), 102 (background), Brian Milne/**First Light**; 21 (middle left), 60 (top), Robert Semeniuk/**First Light**; 21 (bottom right), Wayne Wegner/**First Light**; 21 (bottom left), 56, 79 (top left), 80 (right), 85 (middle), Patrick Morrow/**First Light**; 23 (top/PA 26185), 33 (C 15244), 34 (PA 138573), 41 (C 37966), 49 (C 75818), 59 (top left/PA 3862), 116 (top/PA 37915), 117 (middle top/PA 47245), **Public Archives of Canada**; 23 (bottom left) Derek Trask/**The Stock Market Inc., Toronto**; 24, 25, 28-29, 38, 39, 42, 43 (both), 44 (top and top right), 45 (inset), 47, 49 (inset), 53 (both), 54 (right), 69, **Glenbow Archives**; 31 (both), **National Museums of Canada**; 35, **Confederation Life, Toronto**; 36-37, **RCMP Archives**; 44 (left and bottom right), 45, 46 (all), 59 (top right), 66 (left), 84 (top right), 116 (middle bottom and bottom), 117 (top, middle bottom and bottom), 118 (all), 119 (top, middle top and bottom), 120 (top, middle top and middle bottom), **Provincial Archives of Alberta**; 50, 113 (right), **Henry Kalen**; 54 (left), **B.C. Archives**; 61 (left), 63 (top right), 68 (inset), 79 (bottom left), Mia & Klaus/**Superstock**; 63 (top left) Unlimited Collections/**Superstock**; 66 (right) Robert Knight/**First Light**; 68 (bottom) Harold Clarke/**The Stock Market Inc., Toronto**; 71 (top) **Metro Toronto Library Board**; 74 Marilyn Jackson/**Theatre Calgary**; 74 (inset), **Alberta Ballet Company**; 76, **Trudi Lee**; 77, Luther Linkhart/**Superstock**; 82 (top right), **Courtesy of Illingworth Kerr**; 82 (middle left), Lauren Dale/**Courtesy of Alberta Foundation for the Arts**; 84 (left and bottom right), **Brad Watson**; 85 (inset), 116 (middle top), 119 (middle bottom), 120 (bottom), **Athlete Information Bureau, Ottawa**; 91 (top right), G. Petersen/**First Light**; 94, 114, R. Hartmier/**First Light**; 96 (bottom left) Ken Straiton/**First Light**; 96 (bottom right), Todd Korol/**First Light**; 97, Ron Dahlquist/**Superstock**; 98 (bottom right), Dawn Goss/**First Light**; 100 (top), C. Wershler/**FotoLex**; 105, Shostal Associates/**Superstock**; 110 (inset), Edward Wickson/**Superstock**; 115, Steve Fidler/**Superstock**.